# 21 DAYS
## PROGRAM FOR SELF LOVE

*Three weeks journey to personal transformation*

### SHARAD VERMA

**From the Bestselling author of
"21 SONGS OF SELF LOVE"**

**BLUEROSE PUBLISHERS**
India | U.K.

Copyright © Sharad Verma 2024

All rights reserved by author. No part of this publication may be reproduced, stored in a retrieval system or transmitted in any form or by any means, electronic, mechanical, photocopying, recording or otherwise, without the prior permission of the author. Although every precaution has been taken to verify the accuracy of the information contained herein, the publisher assume no responsibility for any errors or omissions. No liability is assumed for damages that may result from the use of information contained within.

BlueRose Publishers takes no responsibility for any damages, losses, or liabilities that may arise from the use or misuse of the information, products, or services provided in this publication.

For permissions requests or inquiries regarding this publication, please contact:

BLUEROSE PUBLISHERS
www.BlueRoseONE.com
info@bluerosepublishers.com
+91 8882 898 898
+4407342408967

ISBN: 978-93-5819-846-1

Cover design: Tahira
Typesetting: Tanya Raj Upadhyay

First Edition: October 2024

*Dedication*

*This book is dedicated to my parents*

# Acknowledgements

Many people have helped me write this book. After I published my collection of 21 poems - "21 Songs of Self Love" - many readers told me how the book had touched various aspects of their lives. They encouraged me to write a book that would help readers develop self-love at a deeper level. I am grateful to my family, colleagues and many friends who were instrumental in this process - inviting me to give talks and encouraging me to have conversations where I could explore these topics in greater depth. I am also grateful to my family for always encouraging my creativity.

# How to use this book

This book has been designed as a set of exercises to be completed in 21 days. Exercises for each day would typically require two to three hours to complete. However, this may not be possible for most people who have several demands on their time. Therefore, the book can be thought of as a set of 21 exercises which can be completed in a self-paced manner, going at the reader's pace. The exercises need not be done sequentially, and you can start with any topic you find interesting. The last topic is, in many ways, a summation of all the preceding topics, so it is best to be done at the end.

The real benefit of the book lies in completing the exercises and spending time reflecting on the 21 topics of self-love that are instrumental in personal transformation. Exercises have been designed to be practical, simple, and meaningful. You will sometimes find similar exercises at the end of various chapters, although as far as possible, I have tried to design unique exercises and questions. Similarity in exercises occurs because some are relevant to more than one topic. The aim of the book is to bring about a lasting change in our lives with a deep appreciation for self-love and to experience its transformative power for all those whose lives we touch.

The exercises provide both takeaway points and actionable items that can be implemented for experiencing inner change.

You don't have to complete all the exercises provided in each chapter. Choosing the ones that make the most sense to you and those you can relate to are the best picks. Some require more effort than the others.

The questions provided within each chapter are meant to:

1. Provide a quick check-in on your current practice of this aspect
2. Provide reflection and food for thought
3. Encourage strengthening of deeper thinking to bring about change through understanding

Much of this book has been written based on my experiences working with hundreds of people whom I have coached and team members whom I have been fortunate to mentor. It draws from extensive research in 1) psychology and self-help, 2) spirituality - connecting with a higher and deep purpose to live a meaningful life, and 3) neuroscience-based research. At the end of each chapter, I have provided a summary of the neuroscience research from which I have drawn. It is important to note that neuroscience is a rapidly growing field, and sometimes conflicting research findings emerge.

More importantly, the book is intuitive and resonates with what we know to be right based on our inner deeper wisdom.

*Note: This book is not a substitute for professional counselling and medical advice and does not aim to be that. It is advisable to get professional help and counselling and sound medical advice whenever necessary.*

# Table of Contents

Chapter 1  Deeply Valuing Ourselves: The Journey to Self-Love and Personal Growth .................. 1

Chapter 2 Counting our blessings ............................ 32

Chapter 3  Healing from hurt ................................... 48

Chapter 4 Creating and nurturing relationships ......... 63

Chapter 5 Nurturing yourself ................................... 79

Chapter 6 Recognizing the inner voice ..................... 96

Chapter 7 The power of prayer .............................. 116

Chapter 8 Celebrating heartful joy ......................... 136

Chapter 9 Deepest gratitude .................................. 149

Chapter 10 Valuing our gifts .................................. 162

Chapter 11 Change, attachment, letting go ............. 185

Chapter 12 Purpose and meaning ........................... 206

Chapter 13 Believing in yourself ............................ 225

Chapter 14 The power of meditation ...................... 241

Chapter 15 Coping with turbulent thoughts ............ 253

Chapter 16  Connecting with nature ...................... 269

Chapter 17 Dealing with inner conflict .................. 285

Chapter 18 Reflections of a clear mind ................... 296

Chapter 19 Energy, passion, resilience .................... 306

Chapter 20 Experiencing deepest form of love: A Journey to the Heart's Deepest Chamber ................... **319**

Chapter 21 A transformative journey of the soul ...... **331**

# Chapter 1
# Deeply Valuing Ourselves: The Journey to Self-Love and Personal Growth

In the hustle and bustle of our daily lives, we often find ourselves caught up in a whirlwind of responsibilities, expectations, and commitments. Amidst this chaos, it's easy to forget the most important person in our lives: ourselves. Today, I invite you on a transformative journey, one that will guide you towards deeply valuing and nurturing your whole being - your talents, skills, thoughts, body, and soul.

Imagine a world where you wake up each morning, look in the mirror, and see not just your reflection, but a dear friend who deserves love, respect, and care. This is the essence of self-love and self-value. It's not about ego or selfishness; rather, it's about understanding that you are the foundation of your life's experiences. When you treat yourself with kindness and respect, you create a fountain of positivity that overflows into every aspect of your life.

Let's start with your talents and skills. Each of us is a unique combination of abilities, some apparent and others waiting to be discovered. Think of Mohini, a quiet accountant who always believed her worth lay solely in her ability with numbers. One day, encouraged by a friend, she joined a local painting class. To her surprise, she discovered a hidden talent for watercolors. Her paintings not only brought her joy but also connected her with a community of artists. By valuing this newfound skill, Mohini enriched her life in ways she never imagined.

Neuroscience backs up the importance of engaging in activities we enjoy. When we do things we love, our brains release dopamine, a neurotransmitter associated with pleasure and motivation. Dr. Daniel Levitin, a neuroscientist, explains in his book "This Is Your Brain on Music" that engaging in creative activities can reduce anxiety, depression, and even boost immune function. By valuing and nurturing your talents, you're not just having fun; you're actively contributing to your mental and physical well-being.

Now, let's talk about your thoughts. In our digital age, we're bombarded with information and opinions. It's easy to lose sight of our own voice. But your thoughts, your perspective, are invaluable. They are the lens through which you interpret the world. Consider Madan, a young entrepreneur who had a vision for a software product in human resources space. Despite skepticism from investors who thought this was an overcrowded market, Madan trusted his insight. He saw a growing demand for simplification of complex and manual processes in HR. Today, his product is not just profitable but is also influencing the advent of new technology such as Generative AI in human resources.

Neuroscientist Dr. David Eagleman, in his book "The Brain: The Story of You," explains that our perceptions shape our reality. When you value your thoughts, you're more likely to express them and act on them. This not only leads to personal growth but can also inspire change in your community and beyond.

Your body, the vessel that carries you through life, deserves immense respect and care. Yet, in our image-obsessed culture, it's easy to criticize our bodies rather than appreciate them. Consider Prajakta, a mother of two, who struggled with body image after childbirth. She decided to shift her focus. She started thanking her body for carrying her children, for the strength to carry her daily responsibilities, for the energy to play with her kids. This shift in perspective transformed her relationship with her body.

Neuroscience shows us that body image isn't just about looks; it's deeply tied to our mental health. A study published in the journal "Neuron" found that negative self-image can activate the same brain regions as physical pain. Conversely, practices like mindfulness and self-compassion can reduce this activation. By valuing your body, you're not just improving your physical health but also protecting your mental well-being.

And then there's your soul – that intangible essence that makes you, you. It's your values, your passions, your sense of purpose. Tending to your soul means living in alignment with your values. Take Vijay, a CEO who felt drained by his high-stress corporate job. He realized that his work, while lucrative, conflicted with his core value of helping the underprivileged. He took a leap of faith and transitioned to working for a non-government organization. His income dropped, but his sense of fulfilment soared. He found that when your work aligns with your soul's purpose, stress transforms into passion.

Neurologically, living in alignment with your values activates the brain's reward system. A study found that making decisions in line with personal values increased activity in the ventral striatum, an area associated with feelings of reward and motivation. By honoring your soul, you're not just doing what feels right; you're wiring your brain for greater happiness and resilience.

Valuing yourself also means taking ownership of your life. It's easy to feel like a victim of circumstances – a difficult boss, a challenging relationship, or events beyond our control. But true self-value comes from recognizing your power to respond. Viktor Frankl, a psychiatrist and holocaust survivor, beautifully captured this in his book "Man's Search for Meaning." He wrote, "Between stimulus and response there is a space. In that space is our power to choose our response."

Consider Rohini, who lost her job during the pandemic. Initially, she felt helpless and angry. But then she remembered Frankl's words. She chose to see this not as a setback, but as an opportunity to pivot. She'd always dreamed of starting a virtual Yoga teaching service. Within months, her business was thriving, and she felt more in control of her life than ever before.

Neuroscience shows that this sense of control is vital. Studies have found that perceived control activates the prefrontal cortex, the brain's center for planning and decision-making, while reducing activity in the amygdala, our fear center. By taking ownership, you're not just changing your circumstances; you're rewiring your brain for resilience and proactive problem-solving.

Now, let's talk about self-love. It's more than body care and chocolates (though those are lovely, too!). True self-love is about deeply nurturing yourself. It's about setting boundaries, getting enough rest, nourishing your body, and feeding your mind. It's recognizing that you can't pour from an empty cup.

Think of Nitin, a doctor who prided himself on always being there for his patients. But the long hours and emotional toll led to burnout. His performance suffered, and he felt like he was letting everyone down. His mentor encouraged him to prioritize self-care. Nitin started saying no to extra shifts, made time for daily walks, and joined a support group. Not only did his own well-being improve, but he also became a more present, compassionate doctor.

From a neuroscience perspective, self-love is crucial. Chronic stress can shrink the hippocampus, a brain region vital for memory and learning. On the flip side, practices like meditation, exercise, and adequate sleep can increase hippocampal volume. By nurturing yourself, you're not just feeling better in the moment; you're investing in your long-term cognitive health.

Finally, remember that valuing yourself isn't selfish – it's the foundation for caring for others. When you're running on empty, your capacity for empathy and kindness diminishes. But when you're filled with self-love, that love naturally overflows to those around you.

Consider Maria, a teacher who transformed her classroom culture. She started each day with a self-affirmation, reminding herself of her worth and capabilities. Her students noticed the change. Her patience grew, her lessons became more engaging, and her empathy deepened. Soon, her students started practicing self-affirmation too. Test scores improved, bullying decreased, and the classroom became a place of mutual respect.

Neuroscience explains this through the concept of mirror neurons. These neurons fire both when we perform an action and when we observe someone else performing it. When you treat yourself with kindness, your mirror neurons help others learn to do the same. You become a living example of self-love, inspiring those around you.

In conclusion, valuing yourself is not a luxury; it's a necessity. It's the soil in which all your other efforts grow. By cherishing your talents, honoring your thoughts, respecting your body, nurturing your soul, taking ownership of your life, and practicing deep self-care, you set the stage for a life of fulfillment, resilience, and positive impact.

Remember, this journey is not about perfection. There will be days when self-doubt creeps in or when life's demands make self-care feel impossible. But each small step – each moment of self-kindness, each boundary set, each talent nurtured – is a victory. You are worth every ounce of love and respect you give yourself.

So, start today, and every day, look in that mirror and see the incredible, worthy being that you are. Your journey to self-love starts now. And trust me, it's the most important journey you'll ever take.

**Here are 10 actionable takeaways on enhancing your self-value you can easily incorporate into your daily routine:**

1. Daily Affirmations:

Start each day by looking in the mirror and saying something kind to yourself. Example: "I am capable, worthy, and deserving of love." This rewires your brain for positivity, boosting confidence and resilience.

2. Talent Time:

Dedicate 30 minutes daily to a skill or hobby you enjoy, whether it's drawing, playing an instrument, or solving puzzles. This dopamine boost will enhance your mood and cognitive function.

3. Thought Journaling:

Spend 10 minutes each evening writing down your thoughts and insights. This validates your perspective and can lead to innovative ideas. Example: Jot down a workplace challenge and your unique solution.

4. Body Gratitude:

Thank your body daily for what it does, not how it looks. Example: "Thank you, legs, for carrying me through my busy day." This fosters a positive body image and reduces stress.

5. Values Check-In:

Weekly, review if your actions align with your core values. If not, make one small change. Example: If you value learning, sign up for an online course you've been considering.

6. Response Ownership:

When faced with a challenge, pause and ask, "How do I want to respond?" This activates your prefrontal cortex, promoting thoughtful decisions over knee-jerk reactions. Example: Breathe deeply before responding to a critical email.

7. Boundary Setting:

Practice saying "no" to one thing each week that drains you. Example: Decline an invitation to a social event when you need rest. This protects your energy and teaches others to respect your needs.

8. Self-Love Sunday:

Dedicate Sundays (or any day) to rejuvenation. This could mean a nature walk, a nap, or cooking a nourishing meal. Consistent self-care supports cognitive health and emotional balance.

9. Empathy Resonance:

Notice how your self-kindness affects others. Compliment a colleague or listen deeply to a friend. Your mirror neurons will reinforce your own self-love while fostering a culture of kindness.

10. Appreciation At the End of the Day:

Before sleep, list three things you value about yourself from that day. Example: "I was patient with my child, made progress on my project, and took a relaxing bath." This promotes restful sleep and positive self-regard.

**20 questions for self-reflection, each helps you deeply consider your journey of self-value:**

1. How often do I speak kindly to myself, and what impact does my self-talk have on my mood and actions?

Reflect on the tone and content of your inner dialogue. Do you speak to yourself as you would to a dear friend, or are you more critical? Our self-talk profoundly influences our emotional state and behaviors. Neuroscience shows that positive self-talk can reduce activity in the amygdala, our brain's fear center, while increasing activity in regions associated with self-control and rational thinking. This means that kind self-talk doesn't just feel good; it helps you respond more effectively to challenges. Try to catch negative self-talk this week. Each time you notice it, pause and rephrase it compassionately. Over time, this rewires your brain for greater resilience and self-confidence.

2. When was the last time I fully immersed myself in an activity I love, and how did it affect my overall well-being?

Think about a recent occasion when you lost track of time doing something you enjoy – perhaps painting, gardening, or solving a puzzle. How did you feel during and after? Engaging in activities we love triggers the release of neurotransmitters like dopamine and endorphins, which boost mood and reduce stress. Moreover, these activities often induce a state of 'flow' –

complete absorption that quiets self-critical thoughts. This mental break allows your brain to recharge, enhancing cognitive functions like creativity and problem-solving. Make it a point to schedule regular time for these activities. They're not indulgences; they're investments in your mental health and cognitive resilience.

3. Do I give my own ideas and opinions the same weight as others', and if not, what holds me back?

Consider a recent situation where you had an insight or opinion. Did you voice it, or did self-doubt keep you silent? Our brains are prediction machines, constantly learning from our experiences. If we habitually downplay our thoughts, our brains start to predict that our ideas won't be valued, leading us to self-censor. This not only robs the world of our unique perspectives but also reinforces neural pathways of self-doubt. Remember, your viewpoint is shaped by your unique experiences and knowledge. Even if others disagree, sharing your thoughts exercises your brain's executive functions, enhancing critical thinking and communication skills. Start small: share one idea in your next meeting or discussion. Each time you do, you're teaching your brain that your voice matters.

4. How do I respond to my body's signals of hunger, fatigue, or stress, and what does this say about my respect for my physical self?

Your body constantly communicates with you – a growling stomach, heavy eyelids, tense shoulders. How often do you listen? Ignoring these signals isn't just uncomfortable; it can have neurological consequences. For instance, chronic sleep deprivation can impair the hippocampus, crucial for memory consolidation, while ongoing stress can weaken the brain's ability to regulate emotions.

Conversely, honoring your body's needs strengthens the brain-body connection. This enhanced interoception (internal awareness) is linked to better emotional regulation and decision-making. This week, tune into your body's signals. If you're tired, prioritize sleep. If you're stressed, take a break. Each time you respond to your body's needs, you're reinforcing neural pathways of self-care and body respect.

5. Can I articulate my core values, and do my daily actions align with them? If not, how can I bridge this gap?

Take a moment to list your top three values. Maybe it's integrity, compassion, or personal growth. Now, review your past week. Did your actions reflect these values? Living in alignment with our values isn't just morally satisfying; it's neurologically rewarding. Studies show that value-aligned decisions activate the brain's reward centers, similar to the pleasure of eating your favorite food. Misalignment, conversely, can trigger the anterior cingulate cortex, linked to feelings of discomfort and conflict. To bridge any gaps, start with small, daily choices. If you value learning, spend 15 minutes reading an educational article. If it's compassion, perform one kind act daily. These small steps reinforce neural pathways that make value-aligned living more automatic and rewarding over time.

6. When faced with setbacks, do I view them as personal failures or as opportunities for growth? How does this perspective affect my resilience?

Think about a recent setback – a project that didn't go as planned, or a goal you didn't achieve. Did you berate yourself, or did you look for lessons? Your response matters deeply. A fixed mindset ("I'm a failure") activates brain regions associated with avoidance and negative emotion. In contrast, a growth mindset ("What can I learn from this?") engages the prefrontal cortex, involved in adaptive learning and problem-solving. Neuroscientist Carol Dweck's work shows that praising effort over innate ability can foster this growth mindset. This week, reframe a setback as a "yet" statement. Instead of "I can't do this," try "I can't do this yet." This simple shift signals to your brain that growth is possible, enhancing motivation and resilience.

7. How often do I set and maintain boundaries in my personal and professional life? What are the consequences when I don't?

Boundaries are the invisible fences that protect your emotional and physical energy. Think of a time you said "yes" when you wanted to say "no." Maybe you took on extra work or attended a social event despite needing rest. How did it affect you? Poor boundaries can lead to chronic stress, which neuroscience shows can shrink the prefrontal cortex (crucial for planning and self-control) and enlarge the amygdala (our fear center). This makes future boundary-setting even harder. Conversely, setting healthy boundaries activates the brain's reward system, reinforcing the behavior. It also reduces cortisol (the stress hormone).

8. Do I have a consistent self-care routine, and how does it impact my ability to handle stress and care for others?

Self-care isn't selfish; it's a neurological necessity. Consider a week when you neglected self-care. How did it affect your patience, decision-making, or empathy? Chronic stress without adequate self-care can lead to allostatic load – the wear and tear on your brain and body. This can impair the prefrontal cortex, making emotional regulation and complex problem-solving harder. On the flip side, practices like regular exercise, meditation, or creative hobbies can increase BDNF

(Brain-Derived Neurotrophic Factor), a protein crucial for learning, memory, and mood regulation. It's like fertilizer for your brain cells. Moreover, when you're recharged, your mirror neurons (which help us empathize) function better, enhancing your ability to care for others. This week, commit to one daily self-care practice. It's not indulgent; it's essential brain maintenance.

9. How do I celebrate my achievements, big and small? Does my level of self-recognition match my efforts?

Think of a recent accomplishment – finishing a project, learning a new skill, or even making your bed on a tough day. Did you pause to acknowledge it? Self-recognition isn't just feel-good; it's neurologically powerful. When you celebrate achievements, your brain releases dopamine, reinforcing the neural pathways involved in that success. This makes you more likely to repeat successful behaviors. Moreover, self-recognition activates the posterior cingulate cortex, involved in self-reflection and autobiographical memory. This helps integrate the achievement into your self-narrative, gradually building a more confident, capable self-image. Start a 'win journal.' Each day, write down one thing you did well, no matter how small. Over time, you'll train your brain to notice and value your efforts, fueling a positive cycle of motivation and achievement.

10. In what ways do I compare myself to others, and how does this impact my self-worth?

In our social media age, comparison is constant. Reflect on the last time you felt "less than" after scrolling through Instagram or hearing a colleague's success. These comparisons can trigger the dorsomedial prefrontal cortex, linked to self-evaluation and social cognition. When we perceive ourselves negatively in comparison, it can lead to decreased activity in the striatum (reward center) and increased activity in the amygdala (fear center). This neurological shift can manifest as lowered self-esteem, anxiety, or even depression. The antidote? Self-compassion and realistic perspective. Remind yourself that social media is a highlight reel, not reality. Also, practice self-compassionate self-talk. A study in the journal "Mindfulness" found that self-compassion activates the care-giving system (linked to oxytocin), countering the threat system activated by harsh self-judgment. This week, when comparison strikes, pause and say, "Everyone has their own journey. I'm exactly where I need to be."

11. How does my self-value influence my choice of relationships and how I allow others to treat me?

Consider your closest relationships. Do they uplift you, or do you often feel drained or disrespected? Our self-value is a powerful subconscious filter for who we let into our lives. Neuroscience shows that in healthy relationships, social connection activates the brain's reward system, releasing oxytocin (the "love hormone") which reduces stress and enhances well-being. Conversely, in toxic relationships, the constant stress can dysregulate the hypothalamic-pituitary-adrenal (HPA) axis, leading to chronic anxiety or depression. Fascinatingly, our sense of self-worth is mirrored in the brain regions we use to judge others. If you struggle with self-worth, you might unknowingly choose friends or partners who reinforce that low self-image. This week, assess your relationships. Are they nourishing your growth? If not, setting boundaries or even ending toxic relationships isn't just emotionally healthy - it is protective.

12. When I make a mistake, do I practice self-forgiveness, or do I hold onto self-criticism? How does this affect my learning and growth?

Recall a recent mistake - a missed deadline, a forgotten commitment. Did you berate yourself endlessly, or did you find self-compassion? Self-criticism might feel motivating, but neuroscience disagrees. Harsh self-judgment activates the amygdala and cortisol release, putting your brain in a threat state that hinders learning. You're less likely to take risks or try new strategies, stunting your growth. In contrast, self-forgiveness activates the parasympathetic nervous system (rest-and-digest), reducing stress and opening you up to learning. A study found that self-forgiveness was linked to greater personal growth initiative. It allows you to see mistakes as data, not disasters. This week, when you err, try a self-forgiveness mantra: "I'm human. I'm learning. I forgive myself." Watch how this shift makes you more curious about what went wrong and how to improve, rather than just feeling bad.

13. How often do I express gratitude for my own efforts, resilience, or growth? Does this practice impact my overall sense of self?

Gratitude journals are common, but how often do you thank yourself? Think of a challenge you've overcome – a difficult project, a personal loss. Did you acknowledge your own strength? Self-directed gratitude isn't narcissistic; it is game-changing. It activates the anterior cingulate cortex and medial prefrontal cortex, regions linked to self-referential processing and positive self-regard. This isn't just momentary; it builds a more resilient self-image over time. Moreover, gratitude reduces cortisol levels.

Lower stress means clearer thinking and better emotional regulation. Try this: each night, write down one way you showed up for yourself today. "I'm grateful I persevered through that tough meeting." Over weeks, you'll build a tangible record of your resilience, a powerful antidote to self-doubt.

14. Do I take time to understand and process my emotions, or do I tend to suppress or ignore them? How does this emotional awareness affect my decision-making?

Think of the last time you felt a strong emotion – anger, sadness, joy. Did you pause to understand it, or did you push it aside? Emotional suppression might seem efficient, but it's costly. Studies show it increases activity in the amygdala and insula (linked to negative emotions) while decreasing activity in the prefrontal cortex (reasoning and decision-making). This can lead to more reactive, less thoughtful choices. Conversely, labeling emotions ("I feel frustrated") engages the prefrontal cortex, regulating the amygdala. It's like turning down the volume on emotional reactivity, allowing for clearer thinking. Additionally, understanding your emotions provides valuable data. Sadness might signal a need for connection, anger a violated boundary. This week, try an emotional check-in: pause three times daily to name your feelings. Over time, this practice enhances emotional intelligence, leading to wiser decisions and healthier relationships.

15. In what ways do I use my talents or knowledge to help others, and how does this service reflect back on my own sense of worth?

Reflect on a time you used your skills to help someone - maybe you tutored a colleague or volunteered your expertise. How did it make you feel? Altruism isn't just nice; it's a neural booster. When we help others, it activates the mesolimbic system, our reward pathway, similar to the pleasure of eating chocolate. But there's more: a study found that people who volunteer to help on social projects had lower mortality rates, possibly due to reduced stress and increased sense of purpose. This sense of meaning engages the ventromedial prefrontal cortex, crucial for positive self-regard. It's a beautiful cycle: by valuing your talents enough to share them, you reinforce their value. This week, find one way to use your skills for others. Whether it's helping a neighbor or joining a community project, you'll boost both your self-worth and your neural health.

16. How does my physical environment - my home, workspace, or digital spaces - reflect my level of self-respect?

Look around your living or working space. Is it nurturing and organized, or cluttered and draining? Your environment is an external manifestation of your inner state, and it reciprocally affects your brain. A cluttered space can overload the visual cortex, making it harder for your prefrontal cortex to focus and process information. This can lead to increased cortisol, the stress hormone. Conversely, an organized, personalized space activates the anterior cingulate gyrus, involved in controlling emotions and decision-making. It's like your space is either a cognitive tax or a nurturing ground. Moreover, adding elements that bring joy – a favorite photo, a plant – can boost serotonin, our mood stabilizer. This week, spend 20 minutes daily decluttering or adding joyful elements to your space. It's not just tidying; it's creating an environment that tells your brain, "You matter."

17. Do I regularly challenge myself with new learning experiences? How does this continuous growth mindset influence my self-perception?

Consider the last time you learned something new – a language, a recipe, a tech skill. How did mastering it affect your confidence? Embracing new challenges isn't just character-building; it's brain-building. Learning novel skills increases neurogenesis (the birth of new neurons) and strengthens synaptic connections, particularly in the hippocampus. This enhanced cognitive flexibility makes future learning easier and protects against age-related cognitive decline. More profoundly, overcoming learning hurdles reinforces a growth mindset. Each small victory activates the striatum (reward center), building a positive association with challenge. Over time, your self-narrative shifts from "I can't" to "I can learn." This resilient self-image is invaluable in our fast-changing world. This month, take on one new learning challenge. Whether it's an online course or a new hobby, you're not just gaining a skill; you're reinforcing a brain-friendly, growth-oriented view of yourself.

18. How do I balance asserting my needs with maintaining harmonious relationships? Does this balance reflect my belief in my own worthiness?

Think of a recent situation where your needs clashed with someone else's – maybe you needed quiet time when a friend wanted to talk. How did you handle it? Assertiveness isn't aggression; it's the healthy expression of self-value. When we don't assert our needs, the anterior insula (linked to emotional awareness) registers the discomfort but suppressing it can lead to resentment or burnout. Conversely, assertive communication engages the medial prefrontal cortex (self-affirmation) and the anterior cingulate cortex (conflict resolution). It's a balancing act of self-respect and social awareness. Interestingly, people who believe in their worth are more likely to use "and" language: "I value our friendship and I need some alone time." This linguistic choice activates both self-affirmation and social bonding neural networks. This week, practice asserting one need daily. "I appreciate your idea and I'd like to share mine too."

You'll find that respecting your needs often deepens, rather than damages, relationships.

19. When I achieve a goal, do I immediately move on to the next, or do I take time to internalize the success? How does this pattern affect my sense of progress and satisfaction?

Consider your last achievement – a project completed, a fitness goal met. Did you pause to savor it, or quickly set the next target? In our fast-paced world, it's easy to stay on the hamster wheel of achievement without truly internalizing our successes. This constant forward motion can lead to a phenomenon neuroscientists call "hedonic adaptation" – where even significant achievements stop bringing joy. It's because we're not giving our brains the chance to consolidate these wins into our self-narrative. Taking time to reflect on achievements activates the hippocampus and medial prefrontal cortex, helping integrate these experiences into long-term memory and self-concept. This isn't just feel-good; it builds a reservoir of self-efficacy that fuels future efforts. This month, after each achievement, spend 10 minutes journaling about what you learned, how you grew. You're not just logging successes; you're building a more confident, resilient neural architecture.

20. If I could send a message to my brain reinforcing my self-worth, what would it be, and how might internalizing this message change my life trajectory?

Imagine you have a direct line to your neural networks. What would you say to reinforce your inherent worth? Maybe: "You are valuable, capable, and deserving of love, simply because you exist." This isn't mere positive thinking; it's rewiring your brain's foundational beliefs. Repeated positive self-messages can actually alter gene expression in brain cells, promoting factors like BDNF that enhance neural plasticity and resilience. It's like giving your brain the optimal conditions to learn, grow, and bounce back. Moreover, this core belief in your worth becomes a cognitive filter. Challenges become opportunities, not threats. Relationships become collaborations, not validations. Your career becomes an expression of your gifts, not a quest for approval. By consistently sending this message, you're not just feeling better; you're literally shaping a brain primed for a life of authenticity, resilience, and meaningful impact. So, write your message. Read it daily. Let it become the whisper behind every thought. Your brain is listening, and your life will transform.

In these questions, we've journeyed through the neuroscience of self-worth – how valuing yourself isn't just an emotional luxury, but a biological imperative. Your thoughts, habits, and choices are continuously sculpting your neural landscape. By practicing self-kindness, embracing growth, honoring your needs, and recognizing your inherent value, you're not just uplifting your mood. You're building a brain optimized for resilience, creativity, and profound well-being.

Remember, this journey of self-value isn't about perfection. It's about consistent, compassionate effort. Each time you affirm your worth, savor an achievement, or honor a need, you're laying down neural pathways that make self-love more automatic. Over time, this inner shift will radiate outward, enhancing your relationships, work, and overall life satisfaction.

You are, quite literally, the architect of your brain's reality. With every self-valuing thought and action, you're constructing a neural home of self-worth – a place of strength, peace, and limitless potential. It's from this place that you'll not only thrive but also contribute your unique gifts to the world.

This is the journey where your brain, your heart, and the world await the fullest expression of your valued, cherished self.

**Summary of Neuroscience Research in Chapter 1: Deeply Valuing Ourselves - A Journey to Self-Love and Personal Growth**

1. Engaging in creative activities can reduce anxiety, depression, and boost immune function (Dr. Daniel Levitin, "This Is Your Brain on Music").

2. Our perceptions shape our reality (Dr. David Eagleman, "The Brain: The Story of You").

3. Negative self-image can activate the same brain regions as physical pain (study published in the journal "Neuron").

4. Living in alignment with personal values increases activity in the ventral striatum, an area associated with feelings of reward and motivation.

5. Perceived control activates the prefrontal cortex (planning and decision-making center) while reducing activity in the amygdala (fear center).

6. Chronic stress can shrink the hippocampus, a brain region vital for memory and learning.

7. Practices like meditation, exercise, and adequate sleep can increase hippocampal volume.

8. Mirror neurons fire both when we perform an action and when we observe someone else performing it, facilitating learning and empathy.

9. Positive self-talk can reduce activity in the amygdala while increasing activity in regions associated with self-control and rational thinking.

10. Engaging in enjoyable activities triggers the release of neurotransmitters like dopamine and endorphins, boosting mood and reducing stress.

11. Chronic sleep deprivation can impair the hippocampus, crucial for memory consolidation.

12. Enhanced interoception (internal awareness) is linked to better emotional regulation and decision-making.

13. Value-aligned decisions activate the brain's reward centers, similar to the pleasure of eating favorite food.

14. Misalignment with values can trigger the anterior cingulate cortex, linked to feelings of discomfort and conflict.

15. A fixed mindset activates brain regions associated with avoidance and negative emotion, while a growth mindset engages the prefrontal cortex, involved in adaptive learning and problem-solving (Carol Dweck's work).

16. Poor boundaries can lead to chronic stress, which can shrink the prefrontal cortex and enlarge the amygdala.

17. Chronic stress without adequate self-care can lead to allostatic load – the wear and tear on your brain and body.

18. Regular exercise, meditation, or creative hobbies can increase BDNF (Brain-Derived Neurotrophic Factor), a protein crucial for learning, memory, and mood regulation.

19. Celebrating achievements releases dopamine, reinforcing neural pathways involved in success.

20. Self-recognition activates the posterior cingulate cortex, involved in self-reflection and autobiographical memory.

21. Social comparisons can trigger the dorsomedial prefrontal cortex, linked to self-evaluation and social cognition.

22. Self-compassion activates the care-giving system (linked to oxytocin), countering the threat system activated by harsh self-judgment (study in the journal "Mindfulness").

23. In healthy relationships, social connection activates the brain's reward system, releasing oxytocin which reduces stress and enhances well-being.

24. Toxic relationships can dysregulate the hypothalamic-pituitary-adrenal (HPA) axis, leading to chronic anxiety or depression.

25. Harsh self-judgment activates the amygdala and cortisol release, putting the brain in a threat state that hinders learning.

26. Self-forgiveness activates the parasympathetic nervous system (rest-and-digest), reducing stress and opening up to learning.

27. Self-directed gratitude activates the anterior cingulate cortex and medial prefrontal cortex, regions linked to self-referential processing and positive self-regard.

28. Gratitude reduces cortisol levels by up to 23% (unspecified study).

29. Emotional suppression increases activity in the amygdala and insula while decreasing activity in the prefrontal cortex.

30. Labeling emotions engages the prefrontal cortex, regulating the amygdala.

31. Altruism activates the mesolimbic system, the brain's reward pathway.

32. A cluttered space can overload the visual cortex, making it harder for the prefrontal cortex to focus and process information.

33. An organized, personalized space activates the anterior cingulate gyrus, involved in controlling emotions and decision-making.

34. Learning novel skills increases neurogenesis and strengthens synaptic connections, particularly in the hippocampus.

35. Assertive communication engages the medial prefrontal cortex (self-affirmation) and the anterior cingulate cortex (conflict resolution).

36. Reflecting on achievements activates the hippocampus and medial prefrontal cortex, helping integrate experiences into long-term memory and self-concept.

37. Repeated positive self-messages can alter gene expression in brain cells, promoting factors like BDNF that enhance neural plasticity and resilience.

## Chapter 2
## Counting our blessings

In a world that constantly beckons us to strive for more - more money, more success, more possessions - it's all too easy to lose sight of what truly matters. The endless cycle of wanting can be utterly exhausting if we don't take intentional pauses to simply appreciate what we already have.

That's why the practice of counting our blessings is so powerful and transformative. When we mindfully reflect on the goodness present right here, right now, everything shifts. Suddenly, our perspective cracks open to the overflowing abundance that exists all around us, waiting to be noticed and received with humble gratitude.

I know this intimately because I've witnessed the profound impact of this practice in my own life. Many years ago, I hit a period of feeling constantly stressed, overwhelmed, and frankly a bit jaded about the daily grind. It wasn't until a close friend lovingly called me out and suggested keeping a simple gratitude journal that I realized how much I had been taking for granted. Each morning, I slowly began redirecting my focus toward the miracles and gifts, big and small, that graced my life daily. From incredible loved ones to nature's beauty to my home and job, there was always something to appreciate when I made the conscious choice to look.

In cultivating that gratitude muscle, everything became vibrant again. I felt more present, more content, more in awe of this human experience we share. My stress and anxieties diminished as I realized just how much was already good in my world. These days, counting my blessings isn't just a practice but a way of being that keeps me anchored in what's good.

Over time, I have written more than 20,000 gratitude notes. Here is what I have learnt in embracing this practice:

- Initially, we look for big things that we are grateful for
- Gradually, we become observant of small things that we overlook or take for granted
- It is easy to be grateful for things that have been beneficial to us, but the real practice evolves when we are thankful for the adversities that come our way - circumstances that are unpleasant and difficult to deal with. With a grateful heart, we learn to appreciate the vital lessons that adversities bring

I've seen this same beautiful transformation in others too. Take Vidisha (name changed), who after losing her husband in a tragic accident, felt consumed by grief and resentment toward a universe that felt profoundly unfair. It wasn't until a caring counsellor suggested creating a "Book of Blessings" where she listed out everything and everyone she had to be thankful for that the heavy fog began to lift. Filling those pages with memories, people and moments allowed Vidisha to stop fixating on what was lost, and instead cherish and honor the precious lifetime of gifts she did get to experience with her beloved partner. Her book became a reminder that love is truly the richest blessing of all.

Or think about Malti, a first-generation high school student who grew up in a low-income neighborhood – her mother had to work as a maid in many households and save every penny to make both ends meet. For survival, Malti learned to have a scarcity mindset, always feeling like she lacked and had to push, strive, and overcompensate to make up for everything she didn't have. It wasn't until her teacher challenged her to start a gratitude jar that Malti's whole outlook began to change. Each day, she'd add a slip of paper listing out one thing she felt blessed to have or experience that day. Within months, that jar overflowed with an abundance of "blessings" large and small - from home-cooked meals to family bonding to opportunities to learn. Counting those blessings revealed that Malti's life already contained incredible richness, despite not having material things. Her mentality shifted from lacking to feeling like one of the happiest people on earth.

These stories are powerful reminders that amidst any circumstance, challenge, or painful transition, there is always, always something to be grateful for if we choose to zoom in and focus our lens. When we make space to truly count the blessings surrounding us each day, our hearts can't help but overflow with appreciation, joy, and humble reverence for this sacred life we've been given.

So consider this your invitation to start today. Perhaps it's keeping a simple gratitude journal or taking a weekly walk while recounting all you have to be thankful for. Maybe it's creating a "blessings basket" where your family adds notes of gratefulness to read together. Or simply building a new habit of pausing to count your blessings each morning and night.

However you choose to do it, make the commitment to yourself to actively notice the goodness present right here, right now. Because amid all the striving, lack will never be anything but a mentality when you realize just how much you've already been given.

**10 actionable insights on counting your blessings:**

1. Set a daily reminder to pause and list 3-5 things you're grateful for:

Example: Every morning, before checking emails, list gratitude for health, a comfortable bed, and a new day's opportunities. This practice activates the brain's reward system, releasing dopamine and serotonin, which enhance mood and motivation.

2. Look for small, unexpected "blessings" in each day (a cool breeze, a stranger's smile):

Example: Notice a vibrant sunset during your commute. Appreciating such moments engages the prefrontal cortex, responsible for mindfulness, reducing activity in the amygdala, our brain's stress center.

3. Write a gratitude letter to someone who has positively impacted your life:

Example: Thank your high school teacher for believing in you. Writing and delivering such letters increases neural modulation by the neurotransmitter GABA - Gamma-aminobutyric acid, which can have anti-anxiety effects similar to meditation.

4. Create a gratitude jar, box, or bowl to collect written-down blessings:

Example: Write "enjoyed a fun game night with family" on a slip and add it to your jar. This visual reminder of blessings can stimulate the hippocampus in our brain, enhancing memory of positive experiences. Like many parts of the brain's limbic system, the hippocampus is involved in memory, learning, and emotion. Its largest job is to hold short-term memories and transfer them to long-term storage in our brains. It also plays a role in emotional processing, including anxiety.

5. At weekly celebrations, take turns sharing what you're grateful for:

Example: At Sunday dinners, share gratitude for the week's achievements. This communal practice strengthens social bonds, stimulating oxytocin release, the "love hormone" that promotes trust and connection.

6. Make it a mealtime tradition to state something you're blessed to have:

Example: Before lunch, express thanks for nutritious food. This mindful eating practice engages the insula, a brain region linked to bodily awareness and empathy, potentially reducing overeating. Insula or insular cortex is a part of brain that plays a role in cognition, emotions, movement and homeostasis.

7. Express gratitude for your body through loving movement or kind self-talk:

Example: Thank your legs after a walk. Self-compassion activates the ventral striatum and septal area, regions associated with self-soothing and reduced self-criticism.

8. Build a playlist of songs that help you feel appreciative and present:

Example: Music can trigger the nucleus accumbens, part of the reward system, amplifying feelings of gratitude and joy.

9. Take monthly photo or videos of seemingly small blessings you're grateful for:

Example: Capture your pet's funny antics. Reviewing these moments later reactivates the visual cortex, reinforcing positive emotional memories.

10. Gift someone stickies, journals, or art supplies for their own gratitude practice:

Example: Give your friend a beautiful gratitude journal. Acts of kindness activate the brain's pleasure circuits, creating a "helper's high" that can inspire the recipient's gratitude practice.

## 20 Self-Reflection Questions on Gratitude:

1. Do I consistently set aside time each day for gratitude reflection?

Explanation: Consistent gratitude practice, like daily meditation, can reshape neural pathways. Neuroscientist Richard Davidson found that regular meditation increases activity in the left prefrontal cortex, associated with positive emotions and resilience. Similarly, daily gratitude reflection may strengthen these "happiness" circuits.

2. How often do I verbally express gratitude to others?

Explanation: Verbal gratitude expression involves the brain's language centers (Broca's and Wernicke's areas) and emotional processing regions (amygdala, insular cortex). This combination may deepen the emotional impact of gratitude, as seen in studies where gratitude journaling enhanced by sharing led to greater increases in happiness.

3. Can I find gratitude in challenging situations?

Explanation: This ability relates to cognitive reappraisal, a process involving the prefrontal cortex that helps reframe negative events. A study by UCLA's Mindfulness Awareness Research Center showed that gratitude practice can increase grey matter volume in this area, potentially enhancing resilience.

4. Do I appreciate small, everyday things (like a warm cup of coffee)?

Explanation: Appreciating small pleasures engages mindfulness, which, according to Harvard research, can thicken the prefrontal cortex and reduce the amygdala's size. This suggests improved attention to present joys and reduced stress reactivity.

5. How has gratitude helped me overcome past difficulties?

Explanation: Recalling gratitude in tough times involves the hippocampus, crucial for memory. Studies show gratitude can counteract the hippocampal shrinkage caused by chronic stress, potentially aiding in resilience and positive memory retrieval.

6. Am I grateful for my own qualities and achievements?

Explanation: Self-gratitude involves self-compassion, which activates the care-giving system (oxytocin, ventral striatum). A study by Dr Kristin Neff, (a pioneer in self-compassion research) found self-compassion linked to lower anxiety and depression, suggesting self-gratitude could buffer against negative self-judgment.

7. Do I focus more on what I have or what I lack?

Explanation: Focus dictates neural activation. Dwelling on lack can engage the amygdala (threat detection) and anterior cingulate cortex (conflict monitoring), inducing stress. Conversely, gratitude engages the ventral striatum (reward), potentially shifting focus from scarcity to abundance.

8. How does expressing gratitude affect my relationships?

Explanation: Gratitude in relationships boosts oxytocin, the "bonding hormone." A study found gratitude expression increased activity in the medial prefrontal cortex, a region linked to learning and decision-making in social contexts.

9. Do I feel grateful for people in my life, even when they're imperfect?

Explanation: This involves cognitive empathy (understanding others' perspectives), linked to the temporoparietal junction. A gratitude intervention study showed increased activity here, suggesting gratitude might enhance understanding and acceptance of others' flaws.

10. Can I find gratitude in nature and my surroundings?

Explanation: Nature gratitude engages the parasympathetic nervous system ("rest-and-digest"). A University of Berkeley study found appreciation of nature increased better emotional regulation and well-being.

11. How does gratitude influence my attitude towards work or study?

Explanation: Work gratitude can boost dopamine and motivate the brain's executive functions (prefrontal cortex). A study in the Journal of Personality found gratitude predicted greater goal attainment and perseverance, suggesting enhanced work focus and satisfaction.

12. Do I keep a gratitude journal or log?

Explanation: Journaling involves the hippocampus (memory) and Broca's area (language). A study found gratitude journaling increased participants' exercise levels and optimism, indicating potential benefits for physical health and future outlook.

13. How does gratitude impact my physical and mental health?

Explanation: Gratitude reduces cortisol (stress hormone) and increases heart rate variability (HRV), a marker of cardiovascular health. A University of California study found grateful people had better sleep quality, likely due to reduced worry (less amygdala activity) before bed.

14. Am I grateful for lessons learned from past mistakes?

Explanation: Learning from mistakes involves the anterior cingulate cortex (error detection) and dorsolateral prefrontal cortex (cognitive control).

Gratitude for lessons might enhance this process, as suggested by a study where gratitude was linked to better decision-making.

15. Do I feel gratitude for basic necessities (food, shelter, health)?

Explanation: Appreciating basics activates the insula (interoception, empathy). A Max Planck Institute study found insula activation during gratitude correlated with prosocial behavior, suggesting basic gratitude might foster broader social awareness and kindness.

16. How does gratitude affect my spending habits?

Explanation: Gratitude may reduce activity in the nucleus accumbens during tempting purchases, as it's less aroused by materialistic rewards. A Northeastern University study found grateful people were more patient with financial decisions, indicating better impulse control.

17. Do I share my gratitude practice with others?

Explanation: Sharing engages mirror neurons, allowing others to "catch" your gratitude. A University of California study found those who kept gratitude journals were more likely to help others, suggesting a "gratitude contagion" effect.

18. Can I find gratitude even on "bad" days?

Explanation: This involves cognitive flexibility, linked to the lateral prefrontal cortex. A study found regular gratitude practice increased grey matter here, potentially enhancing the ability to find silver linings in adversity.

19. How does gratitude influence my future outlook?

Explanation: Optimism involves the rostral anterior cingulate cortex and amygdala. An Indiana University study found gratitude practice led to lasting changes in these areas months later, suggesting enduring benefits for mood and outlook.

20. Am I cultivating an environment of gratitude in my home, work, or community?

Explanation: Group gratitude can synchronize brain activity (measured by EEG) in regions like the temporoparietal junction, enhancing empathy and cooperation. A University of Oregon study found group gratitude rituals increased collective problem-solving and cohesion.

These questions, grounded in neuroscience, can deepen your understanding of how gratitude shapes your brain, behavior, and relationships, motivating a richer practice of counting your blessings.

**List of all Neuroscience Research in Chapter 2: Counting our blessings**

1. Gratitude practice activates the brain's reward system, releasing dopamine and serotonin, which enhance mood and motivation.

2. Appreciating small moments engages the prefrontal cortex, responsible for mindfulness, reducing activity in the amygdala, the brain's stress center.

3. Writing and delivering gratitude letters increase neural modulation by the neurotransmitter GABA (Gamma-aminobutyric acid), which can have anti-anxiety effects similar to meditation.

4. Visual reminders of blessings can stimulate the hippocampus, enhancing memory of positive experiences.

5. Communal gratitude practices stimulate oxytocin release, the "love hormone" that promotes trust and connection.

6. Mindful eating practices engage the insula, a brain region linked to bodily awareness and empathy, potentially reducing overeating.

7. Self-compassion activates the ventral striatum and septal area, regions associated with self-soothing and reduced self-criticism.

8. Music can trigger the nucleus accumbens, part of the reward system, amplifying feelings of gratitude and joy.

9. Reviewing positive moments reactivates the visual cortex and amygdala, reinforcing positive emotional memories.

10. Acts of kindness activate the brain's pleasure circuits, creating a "helper's high."

11. Neuroscientist Richard Davidson found that regular meditation increases activity in the left prefrontal cortex, associated with positive emotions and resilience.

12. UCLA's Mindfulness Awareness Research Center showed that gratitude practice can increase grey matter volume in the prefrontal cortex, potentially enhancing resilience.

13. Harvard research suggests mindfulness can thicken the prefrontal cortex and reduce the amygdala's size, improving attention to present joys and reducing stress reactivity.

14. Studies show gratitude can counteract hippocampal shrinkage caused by chronic stress, potentially aiding in resilience and positive memory retrieval.

15. A study found gratitude expression increased activity in the medial prefrontal cortex, a region linked to learning and decision-making in social contexts.

16. A gratitude intervention study showed increased activity in the temporoparietal junction, suggesting gratitude might enhance understanding and acceptance of others' flaws.

17. A University of California study found grateful people had better sleep quality, likely due to reduced worry (less amygdala activity) before bed.

18. A Max Planck Institute study found insula activation during gratitude correlated with prosocial behavior.

19. A Northeastern University study found grateful people were more patient with financial decisions, indicating better impulse control.

20. An Indiana University study found gratitude practice led to lasting changes in the rostral anterior cingulate cortex and amygdala, suggesting enduring benefits for mood and outlook.

21. A University of Oregon study found group gratitude rituals increased collective problem-solving and cohesion, potentially through synchronized brain activity in regions like the temporoparietal junction.

# Chapter 3
# Healing from hurt

Hurt is part of being human. Disappointments, heartbreaks, betrayals - they happen to all of us at some point or another.

Hurt cuts deep sometimes. Feeling like the pain will never end. Like part of you has been torn out and damaged beyond repair. It's brutal. And it's okay to fully feel all of those feelings when life deals you a crushing blow.

But here's what I've learned - we don't have to stay stuck in that pain forever. Healing is always possible if we choose to walk that path, one brave step at a time. It won't happen overnight, but little by little, the sharpness can start to dull.

I'm not saying it's easy. Healing from hurt might just be one of the hardest yet most important inner journeys we'll ever take. It requires feeling it all to get through it. It demands looking inward with ruthless honesty. And it means summoning incredible reserves of self-compassion.

Yet this work is also sacred. Because when we heal our hurt, we reclaim our power. We let go of what doesn't serve us. We transform pain into inner strength and wisdom. Most importantly, we open up space to fully experience joy again.

I've witnessed this firsthand. Like with Sumana - a woman who had her trust shattered when she discovered her husband's affair. At first, Sumana was consumed by betrayal, anger, and devastation. But over time, she learned to let those emotions combust through journaling, counseling, and being lovingly held by friends. As she healed, that fury transformed into self-respect and boundaries. What could have made her bitter instead left Sumona empowered, valuing herself deeply.

Then there's Mahesh, who endured years of childhood abuse before finally getting free. His path to healing has been gnarly - processing intense trauma, brutal triggers, and a tsunami of big feelings. But by courageously feeling it all through therapy and breathwork, Mahesh has stopped letting his past define him. He's rewriting the narratives of shame and harm, and building an identity of resilience and self-love.

Maybe you're like Aruna, carrying invisible wounds from a lifetime of oppressive systems and injustice. Cultural traumas can leave us hurting in ways that get minimized or overlooked. But Aruna has found incredible strength and community in joining group healings and doing the work to unpack generational pains. Connecting with her roots while setting healthy boundaries around what she'll no longer tolerate.

I could go on and on because each person's journey is unique. But the common thread is this - we all have the capacity to transform our hurt into something meaningful and powerful, as long as we stay committed to the process of working through it with self-compassion.

Will it be messy and nonlinear? 100%. Some days will feel like backsliding. Other days will bring profound breakthroughs. All of it is part of the path forward.

So if you're struggling with hurt today, take heart. Healing is always possible for those willing to tenderly feel it all to let it all go. From that place, you can create a life of deeper authenticity, boundaries and self-respect.

One step at a time, you've got this.

**Here are 10 Actionable Ways to Heal from Hurt:**

1. Brain dumping: Unfiltered expression of thoughts and feelings through journaling, voice notes, or drawing helps process emotions. This practice engages the prefrontal cortex, responsible for executive functions, allowing you to observe and regulate emotions more effectively. Example: Jotting down anger after a hurtful comment helps release pent-up emotions.

2. Coping strategies: Techniques like breathwork and mindfulness engage the parasympathetic nervous system, reducing stress responses. They allow you to fully experience emotions without judgment, fostering self-acceptance. Example: Using deep breathing during anxiety activates the vagus nerve, calming the amygdala (fear center) and promoting a sense of safety.

3. Professional help: Methods like EMDR, somatic therapy, and inner child work help process traumas, reducing their emotional charge. Example: A counselor guiding you through childhood abandonment issues can help rewire neural pathways associated with that trauma.

4. Physical release: Exercise, dance, or shaking releases endorphins and reduces cortisol (stress hormone). Physical movement also helps process emotions stored in the body. Example: Dancing to upbeat music can release sadness.

5. Unsent letter: Writing an unsent letter engages the left brain (logical) and right brain (emotional), facilitating emotional processing. Burning or burying it symbolizes letting go. Example: Writing to a former friend who betrayed you allows you to articulate your pain, aiding in acceptance and closure.

6. Self-compassionate mantras: Repeating mantras activates the anterior cingulate cortex and insula, regions associated with self-compassion. This counteracts the inner critic's harsh voice. Example: Saying "I'm doing my best" after a mistake helps shift from self-judgment to self-kindness, reducing cortisol levels.

7. Support groups: Sharing authentically in a group activates mirror neurons, fostering empathy and connection. This reduces feelings of isolation. Example: Joining a group for survivors of narcissistic abuse can validate your experiences and provide strategies for healing.

8. Rituals and ceremonies: Rituals engage the limbic system, helping process emotions symbolically. They create a sense of closure and new beginnings.

9. Joy and presence: Positive experiences strengthen neural pathways associated with wellbeing. Focusing on joy activates the reward system (dopamine). Example: Noticing the warmth of sunlight on your skin after a

period of depression reinforces that positive feelings are possible.

10. Celebrate milestones: Celebrating wins releases dopamine and serotonin, reinforcing positive behaviors and boosting self-esteem. It also helps reframe your narrative from victim to survivor. Example: Treating yourself to a nature walk after a breakthrough reinforces your commitment to healing.

## 20 Questions to Assess Healing from Past Hurt:

1. Do I catch myself in negative self-talk less often than before? Negative self-talk often stems from the inner critic, a voice shaped by past hurts. As you heal, the anterior cingulate cortex (ACC) becomes more active, enhancing self-compassion. This question helps you notice if you're shifting from self-criticism to self-kindness. Example: If you used to berate yourself for small mistakes but now respond with "I'm learning," it indicates your ACC is overriding the amygdala's fear-based reactions.

2. Am I able to set and maintain healthier boundaries? Boundaries are often compromised due to past hurts. Setting boundaries engages the prefrontal cortex (decision-making) and insula (bodily awareness). This question gauges if you're honoring your needs. Example: If you used to let a toxic friend overstep but now calmly

express your limits, it shows your brain is prioritizing self-care over fear of rejection.

3. Do I feel my emotions more fully without getting overwhelmed? Past hurts can lead to emotional suppression or flooding. Healing involves regulating emotions via the interplay of the amygdala (emotion center) and prefrontal cortex. This question checks if you're moving towards emotional equilibrium. Example: If you can now cry when sad without spiraling into despair, it suggests your prefrontal cortex is effectively regulating the amygdala's response.

4. Have I noticed an increase in moments of joy or contentment? Chronic hurt can dampen positive emotions. As you heal, the brain's reward system (involving dopamine and the nucleus accumbens) becomes more responsive. This question assesses if you're experiencing more positive states. Example: If you find yourself smiling at a bird's song when before you wouldn't have noticed, it indicates your reward system is reactivating.

5. Am I more present in daily life rather than stuck in past hurts? Past trauma can keep us in a state of hypervigilance. Mindfulness activates the insula and ACC, promoting present-moment awareness. This question checks if you're more grounded in the now. Example: If you can enjoy a meal without intrusive

thoughts of past betrayals, it suggests your brain is shifting from survival mode to a state of safety.

6. Do I find it easier to trust and connect with others? Hurt can disrupt the brain's social engagement system, making connection difficult. As you heal, oxytocin (the "bonding hormone") flows more freely. This question gauges if you're opening up to healthy relationships. Example: If you used to avoid friendships but now share vulnerably with a trusted person, it shows oxytocin is facilitating social bonding.

7. Have I noticed my self-care habits improving? Past hurt can lead to self-neglect. Self-care engages the ventromedial prefrontal cortex, associated with self-value. This question checks if you're treating yourself with more kindness. Example: If you used to skip meals when stressed but now make sure to nourish yourself, it indicates your brain is prioritizing your wellbeing.

8. Am I more resilient in facing life's challenges? Trauma can weaken resilience. As you heal, neuroplasticity allows the formation of new, resilient neural pathways. This question assesses if you're bouncing back better. Example: If a job rejection used to trigger a week of despair but now prompts strategic planning, it shows your brain is adapting more flexibly.

9. Do I find myself ruminating less on past hurts? Rumination involves the default mode network (DMN) getting stuck in past-focused loops. Healing involves the executive network interrupting these loops. This question checks if you're less caught in mental time-travel. Example: If thoughts of an ex-partner's betrayal used to consume hours but now pass quickly, your executive network is regulating the DMN more effectively.

10. Have I been able to reframe past hurts into growth opportunities? Hurt can lock us into a victim mindset. Post-traumatic growth involves the dorsolateral prefrontal cortex, crucial for cognitive reappraisal. This question gauges if you're finding wisdom in wounds. Example: If you now see a past job loss as the push you needed for a better career, your brain is reframing adversity constructively.

11. Am I more accepting of my flaws and imperfections? Past criticism can fuel perfectionism. Self-acceptance involves the ventral striatum and ventromedial prefrontal cortex. This question checks if you're embracing your whole self. Example: If you used to hide perceived flaws but now share them openly, it suggests these brain regions are fostering self-acceptance.

12. Do I find myself judging others less harshly? Past hurt can make us project pain onto others. As you heal,

mirror neurons and the temporoparietal junction (involved in empathy) become more active. This question assesses if you're more understanding. Example: If you used to quickly label someone "bad" for a mistake but now consider their struggles, it shows increased empathic processing.

13. Am I more attuned to my body's signals? Trauma can disconnect us from bodily sensations. Healing involves the insula, key for interoception (internal awareness). This question checks if you're more in tune with your body. Example: If you now notice tension in your shoulders when anxious, rather than just feeling "off," your insula is enhancing bodily awareness.

14. Have I noticed an improvement in my sleep patterns? Past hurts can disrupt sleep via the hypothalamic-pituitary-adrenal (HPA) axis. As you heal, the HPA axis regulates better. This question gauges if you're experiencing more restful sleep. Example: If nightmares of past abuse have reduced, allowing deeper sleep, it suggests your HPA axis is normalizing.

15. Do I engage more in activities that truly fulfill me? Hurt can lead to numbing behaviors. Healing involves the nucleus accumbens responding more to intrinsic rewards. This question checks if you're pursuing genuine interests. Example: If you used to binge-watch TV to escape but now spend evenings painting (a longtime

passion), your reward system is valuing authentic fulfillment.

16. Am I able to receive compliments and praise more easily? Past criticisms can make accepting positivity hard. The ventral striatum plays a role in processing praise. This question assesses if you're more open to affirmation. Example: If a compliment on your work used to make you uncomfortable but now brings a sense of pride, your brain is becoming more receptive to positive feedback.

17. Have I noticed a decrease in physical symptoms of stress? Chronic hurt can manifest physically via the autonomic nervous system. Healing balances the sympathetic (fight-or-flight) and parasympathetic (rest-and-digest) systems. This question checks if your body is more at ease. Example: If stress-related migraines have reduced, it suggests your autonomic nervous system is finding balance.

18. Do I find myself more willing to try new things or take positive risks? Past failures can breed avoidance. The ventral tegmental area (VTA) plays a role in motivation and novelty-seeking. This question gauges if you're more open to growth. Example: If you used to avoid public speaking due to past humiliation but now volunteer for presentations, it shows your VTA is motivating you towards challenges.

19. Am I more consistent in my self-compassion practice? Self-compassion can feel foreign after hurt. Regular practice strengthens the neural circuits involving the ACC, insula, and prefrontal cortex. This question checks if self-compassion is becoming habitual. Example: If you now instinctively offer yourself kindness after a setback, rather than having to consciously remember, these circuits are becoming well-worn paths.

20. Do I feel a growing sense of purpose or meaning? Hurt can make life feel meaningless. Finding purpose engages the ventromedial prefrontal cortex and hippocampus (memory center). This question assesses if you're constructing a meaningful life narrative. Example: If you're now mentoring others with similar past hurts, it suggests your brain is weaving your experiences into a larger, purposeful story.

The path to healing is right there within you, waiting to be embraced. Take it one breath, one baby step, one choice at a time. When the hurt breaks you open, dare to use that shattered space as a portal to your most radiant, peaceful self. You're worth it.

# Neuroscience Concepts and Research Quoted in Chapter 3: Healing from hurt

1. Prefrontal cortex: Involved in executive functions, observation, and regulation of emotions.

2. Parasympathetic nervous system: Engaged through techniques like breathwork and mindfulness, reducing stress responses.

3. Amygdala: The brain's fear center, which can be calmed through activation of the vagus nerve.

4. EMDR (Eye Movement Desensitization and Reprocessing): Uses bilateral stimulation to reprocess traumatic memories.

5. Neural pathways: Can be rewired through various therapeutic techniques.

6. Endorphins: Released through physical activities like exercise and dance.

7. Cortisol: Stress hormone that can be reduced through various healing practices.

8. Left and right brain engagement: Facilitated through activities like writing unsent letters.

9. Anterior cingulate cortex (ACC): Associated with self-compassion and can be activated through mantras.

10. Insula: Involved in self-compassion, bodily awareness, and interoception.

11. Mirror neurons: Activated in group settings, fostering empathy and connection.

12. Limbic system: Engaged through rituals and ceremonies, helping to process emotions symbolically.

13. Dopamine and serotonin: Released when celebrating milestones, reinforcing positive behaviors.

14. Nucleus accumbens: Part of the brain's reward system, involved in experiencing positive emotions.

15. Ventromedial prefrontal cortex: Associated with self-value and finding purpose.

16. Default mode network (DMN): Involved in rumination on past events.

17. Executive network: Helps interrupt rumination loops.

18. Dorsolateral prefrontal cortex: Crucial for cognitive reappraisal in post-traumatic growth.

19. Ventral striatum: Involved in self-acceptance and processing praise.

20. Temporoparietal junction: Involved in empathy.

21. Hypothalamic-pituitary-adrenal (HPA) axis: Regulates sleep patterns and stress responses.

22. Autonomic nervous system: Balances sympathetic (fight-or-flight) and parasympathetic (rest-and-digest) responses.

23. Ventral tegmental area (VTA): Plays a role in motivation and novelty-seeking.

24. Hippocampus: Involved in memory and constructing meaningful life narratives.

## Chapter 4
## *Creating and nurturing heartfelt relationships*

There's a simple yet profound truth about being human that I don't think we can ever be reminded of enough: We need each other.

Not in some vague, philosophical way. But in a soul-deep, hardwired, scientifically-validated sense. Neuroscience shows that our brains are quite literally wired for connection. Relationships shape our neural circuits, driving hormones like oxytocin that reduce anxiety and inflammation. Warm social bonds can boost our immune function and longevity by lowering stress.

But it goes far beyond just physical health benefits. Our relationships provide the fertile soil for us to thrive and bloom into our fullest, most authentic selves. When we feel safe, seen, and celebrated for who we truly are, our hearts start to open. Our creativity and passions flow more freely. Our shadows and growth edges become easier to explore and embrace.

In other words, heartfelt relationships give us the courage and safety to shed all the masks and heavy armor. To feel the full spectrum of being alive without judgment or conditions. To experience all the richness, warmth, joy and growth that comes through entering the tender vulnerability of simply showing up as we are.

I've witnessed this transformative power of human connection up close, time and again. Like with my friend Anushka. After surviving an abusive marriage that left her feeling crushed and small, it was the loving bond with her chosen family that allowed her to start breathing and living fully again. As she soaked up the unconditional acceptance and playful laughter with her soul tribe, something started re-awakening within her - her radiant essence, her voice, her vibrant life force. Slowly but surely, Anushka came back to herself.

Then there's Raman. Growing up in a low-income environment with the odds stacked against him, it was the community of mentors and elders in the neighborhood who gave him experiences of feeling truly valued and worthy. Their intentional, trusted relationships offered a mirror for Raman to recognize his own strength and potential. Years later, those bonds empowered him to break negative cycles and build a life of passion and purpose.

And who could forget about the simple yet profound delight and healing available through intergenerational friendships? Seeing the way lonely seniors in nursing homes light up during visits from kindly neighborhood kids. Or the pure magic of a new grandparent gazing upon their grandchild with revered, unconditional love. These soul-nourishing connections both celebrate where we've been while offering a sacred container for where we're going.

The research only underscores how vital all of this is. One widely cited study found that lack of social connection is a greater risk factor for mortality than obesity, smoking or high blood pressure. Loneliness can be as damaging to our health as smoking 15 cigarettes a day. Conversely, people who feel genuinely supported and cared for enjoy living longer while also reporting a higher degree of life satisfaction and trust.

Clearly, our human need for heartfelt connection is hardwired into our DNA and critical for our psychological and physical wellbeing. And yet, in our modern, isolating world, so many of us feel starved for it. Rates of loneliness continue to rise across all demographics.

You have an immense power inside you through your open heart, your cozy presence, your tender-hearted way of showing up with others. By nurturing authentic relationships rooted in realness and vulnerability, you give one of the greatest gifts - helping others shed the limited stories trapping them so they can more fully blossom into their most generous, joyful, self-expressed selves.

This is the special work. Witnessing one another. Walking alongside each other through the tender and tough seasons. Sharing genuine laughter and breaking bread together. Holding space for the fullness of humanity - from our deepest joys to our wildest dreams to our most gut-wrenching sorrows. Through it all, we feel the richness of being seen, accepted and loved into existence.

So let this be your invitation, your humble but mighty calling, to savor and create more of those kinds of warm, nurturing bonds that help us heal and come home to the wholeness of who we are. It could be brewing a cozy weekly ritual with a dear friend. Or making new connections through community meetups or neighborhood events. Maybe it's reconnecting with long lost family or chosen family. Or cultivating new intergenerational friendships that nourish both sides.

Each act of investing heartfully into genuine relationships is an act of love for you and for this world we all share. Every authentic bond we create or deepen reverberates out in profound ways. It opens channels for people to live with more courage, resilience and freedom. To feel less alone and more supported to shine their light unapologetically.

It's really quite simple, and yet transformative beyond measure. When we show up with tender-hearted care and space for our fellow humans to be all of who they are, we help each other blossom into our most vibrant, expressed selves. We access wells of joy, belonging and meaning hard to find anywhere else in this crazy world. We find the kinship that helps us not only survive, but thrive.

Keep choosing presence over perfection. Keep holding space for connection and vulnerability within yourself and others. It's the pathway to so much richness, healing, warmth and genuine celebration of this miraculous life.

**10 Actionable Ways to Create and Nurture Heartfelt Relationships:**

1. Being thoughtful and considerate: This involves being mindful of others' needs and perspectives. For example, remembering a friend's food preferences when hosting a dinner or offering a listening ear when a loved one is going through a tough time.

2. Understanding deeply and non-judgmentally: Seek to truly comprehend others' experiences, beliefs, and motivations without criticism. Ask open-ended questions and provide a safe space for them to share, rather than making assumptions.

3. Appreciating others: Recognize and value people's unique qualities, strengths, and contributions. Express

gratitude and offer genuine compliments, such as thanking a coworker for their hard work on a project.

4. Building trust: Be reliable, honest, and consistent in your words and actions. Keep confidences and follow through on commitments, such as being on time for appointments or keeping promises made to loved ones.

5. Nurturing love: Cultivate feelings of care, affection, and acceptance towards others. Show warmth, kindness, and support, such as offering a hug or words of encouragement during difficult times.

6. Investing time and quality conversations: Prioritize spending quality time together, engaging in meaningful conversations, and sharing experiences. For example, scheduling regular date nights or weekend outings with friends.

7. Fostering belonging: Make others feel included, valued, and accepted for who they are. Create an environment where they can be their authentic selves, such as in a welcoming social group or family gathering.

8. Promoting mutual understanding: Seek to truly understand others' perspectives, emotions, and experiences. Validate their feelings and show empathy, such as actively listening and reflecting back what you've heard.

9. Contributing to happiness and meaning: Nurture relationships that bring joy, fulfilment, and a sense of purpose to both individuals, such as a close friendship or romantic partnership.

10. Practicing patience and perseverance: Understand that building deep connections takes time and effort. Remain committed and patient throughout the process, even when facing challenges or conflicts.

20 Questions to Assess Caring and Nurturing Heart-Based Relationships:

1. Do you prioritize quality time with the other person, free from distractions, to engage in meaningful conversations and shared experiences?

This question assesses the commitment to fostering deep connections by intentionally carving out dedicated time for meaningful interactions without external distractions. Quality time facilitates understanding, trust, and emotional intimacy.

2. Do you actively listen to the other person without judgment, seeking to understand their perspectives, emotions, and experiences?

Active listening involves fully attending to the other person, suspending judgment, and demonstrating a genuine desire to understand their inner world. It creates a safe space for vulnerability and self-expression.

3. Do you express gratitude and appreciation for the other person's unique qualities, strengths, and contributions?

Expressing gratitude and appreciation reinforces the value and importance of the relationship. It fosters a sense of being seen, understood, and appreciated for one's authentic self.

4. Do you offer empathy and support during challenging times, providing a compassionate and non-judgmental presence?

Empathy and support during difficult times strengthen the emotional bond and create a sense of safety and security within the relationship. It demonstrates care and a willingness to be present for the other person.

5. Do you make efforts to understand the other person's love language and express affection in ways meaningful to them?

Understanding and expressing affection in ways that resonate with the other person's love language (e.g., words of affirmation, quality time, acts of service, etc.) fosters a deeper emotional connection and a sense of being truly seen and valued.

6. Do you create opportunities for shared experiences and adventures, fostering a sense of connection and creating lasting memories?

Shared experiences and adventures create a shared history and strengthen the emotional bond. They provide opportunities for new perspectives, personal growth, and the creation of cherished memories.

7. Do you prioritize open and honest communication, even during difficult conversations, while maintaining respect and empathy?

Open and honest communication, even during challenging discussions, builds trust and intimacy. It demonstrates a willingness to be vulnerable and a commitment to working through conflicts constructively.

8. Do you strive to understand the other person's beliefs, values, and life experiences without judgment or criticism?

Seeking to understand the other person's beliefs, values, and life experiences without judgment creates an environment of acceptance and respect. It fosters a deeper appreciation for their unique perspectives and worldviews.

9. Do you encourage and support the other person's personal growth, dreams, and aspirations?

Encouraging and supporting personal growth, dreams, and aspirations demonstrates a genuine investment in the other person's well-being and fulfilment. It fosters a sense of being valued and believed in.

10. Do you make efforts to maintain a balance between independence and togetherness, respecting each other's need for personal space and autonomy?

Maintaining a balance between independence and togetherness ensures that both individuals feel respected, valued, and able to maintain their sense of self within the relationship.

11. Do you create opportunities for shared laughter, playfulness, and enjoying each other's company in a light-hearted manner?

Shared laughter and playfulness contribute to the joy and positive emotional experiences within the relationship. It promotes a sense of connection, happiness, and emotional well-being.

12. Do you strive to resolve conflicts in a constructive and respectful manner, seeking mutual understanding and compromise?

Constructive conflict resolution involves empathy, active listening, and a willingness to find mutually acceptable solutions. It strengthens trust, intimacy, and the ability to navigate challenges together.

13. Do you make efforts to understand and respect each other's boundaries, needs, and personal preferences?

Respecting boundaries, needs, and personal preferences demonstrates consideration and care for the other person's well-being and autonomy. It fosters a sense of safety and mutual respect within the relationship.

14. Do you create a safe and non-judgmental environment where both individuals can be vulnerable and authentic without fear of criticism or rejection?

A safe and non-judgmental environment promotes vulnerability and authenticity, allowing individuals to fully express their thoughts, feelings, and true selves without fear of rejection or criticism.

15. Do you make an effort to strengthen the emotional intimacy in the relationship? Emotional intimacy refers to the close emotional bond, vulnerability, and sense of deep understanding between two people. It involves sharing innermost thoughts, feelings, fears, and life experiences. Strengthening emotional intimacy requires intentional effort, such as having open and honest conversations about your inner worlds, sharing personal

stories, and actively listening without judgment. It also involves creating a safe space for vulnerability, where both individuals feel comfortable expressing their authentic selves.

16. Do you prioritize open and honest communication about your needs, feelings, and expectations, while also being receptive to the other person's perspectives?

Open and honest communication about needs, feelings, and expectations, coupled with receptivity to the other person's perspectives, fosters mutual understanding, trust, and the ability to address concerns proactively.

17. Do you make efforts to understand and accommodate each other's attachment styles, providing the appropriate level of closeness or independence?

Understanding and accommodating each other's attachment styles (e.g., secure, anxious, avoidant) helps meet emotional needs and fosters a sense of security and comfort within the relationship.

18. Do you create opportunities for shared experiences and adventures that challenge and stretch both individuals, fostering personal growth and creating lasting memories?

Shared experiences and adventures that challenge and stretch both individuals promote personal growth, shared accomplishments, and the creation of lasting memories that strengthen the emotional bond.

19. Do you make efforts to understand and accommodate each other's love languages, ensuring that both individuals feel loved and appreciated in ways meaningful to them?

Understanding and supporting each other's love languages (e.g., words of affirmation, quality time, acts of service, physical touch, gift-giving) ensures that both individuals feel loved and appreciated in ways that resonate with their unique needs and preferences.

20. Do you regularly check in to ensure the relationship remains fulfilling for both people? Relationships are dynamic and ever-evolving, and it's essential to regularly check in with each other to ensure that the relationship remains fulfilling for both individuals. This can involve having open and honest conversations about each person's needs, desires, and concerns, and actively listening to each other's perspectives. It's also important to address any issues or conflicts that may arise in a constructive and respective manner, seeking mutual understanding and compromise.

From a neuroscience perspective, regular check-ins and open communication can help strengthen the neural pathways associated with emotional regulation, empathy, and social cognition. The prefrontal cortex, which is involved in decision-making, emotional intelligence, and understanding others' perspectives, plays a crucial role in maintaining healthy and fulfilling relationships.

Life's trials and blessings aren't meant to be weathered alone. We all crave relationships that allow us to soften into our wholeness - the joy, the hurt, the humanity of being seen. Stay openhearted and keep nurturing the bonds that whisper, "You belong. You're loved. You're home."

**List of Neuroscience Concepts and Research in Chapter 4: Creating and nurturing heartfelt relationships**

1. Neuroscience shows that our brains are wired for connection.

2. Relationships shape our neural circuits, driving hormones like oxytocin that reduce anxiety and inflammation.

3. Warm social bonds can boost our immune function and longevity by lowering stress.

4. Mirror neurons in the brain are activated when we observe others' actions, emotions, and experiences, fostering empathy and understanding.

5. The release of oxytocin, often called the "love hormone," is associated with feelings of bonding, trust, and attachment in relationships.

6. The ventral striatum and other reward regions in the brain are activated when we experience positive social interactions and feelings of belongingness.

7. The amygdala, a key region for processing emotions, plays a role in emotional regulation, conflict resolution, and maintaining healthy relationships.

8. The prefrontal cortex is involved in decision-making, emotional intelligence, and understanding others' perspectives, which are crucial for nurturing heart-based relationships.

9. Regular check-ins and open communication can help strengthen the neural pathways associated with emotional regulation, empathy, and social cognition.

# Chapter 5
# Nurturing yourself

In a world that constantly glorifies hustle and productivity, the much-needed act of nurturing yourself often gets shoved aside. We convince ourselves that self-care is a luxury, an indulgence, something that can wait until we've crossed off every single to-do.

But here's the truth - lovingly attending to your own needs is one of the most radical and important acts of service you can offer this world. Because when you take care of yourself first, you stop operating from a place of depletion, stress and resentment. Instead, you cultivate overflow from a wellspring of peace, presence and self-acceptance to pour into all you do.

I know this firsthand because I've witnessed the profound impacts, both positive and negative, of how we treat ourselves. Years ago, I spent many years running myself low - overworking, putting everyone else's needs first, numbing through unhealthy coping habits. Irritable, anxious, burnt out. My relationships suffered, my creativity tanked, my joy evaporated. It wasn't until I hit a breaking point and started prioritizing basic self-care that I remembered how to actually feel good again.

Once I established a consistent routine of nourishing practices like morning meditation, eating nourishing meals, spending time in nature, and simply giving myself permission to rest, everything shifted. I had more patience, focus, and zest for living. I naturally treated myself and others with more care and authenticity. My light started shining again.

I've seen this same life-giving power of self-nurturing in so many others too. Like Maya, a busy professional and single mom who felt like she spent every waking hour caring for others yet never herself. Stress and overwhelm left her feeling detached and resentful until she finally started blocking off regular "self-care windows" in her schedule. Making those guilt-free appointments to take a yoga class, read for pleasure or simply lay outside and bask in the warm sun gave Maya a chance to rejuvenate her spirit. She soon had more energy, groundedness and capacity to joyfully show up as the mom, friend and businesswoman she wanted to be.

Self-nurturing is vital, regardless of age, gender or social status. Take Vishwanath - raised in a culture that conditions men to suppress their emotions and need for tenderness. For years, Vishwanath walked through life disconnected from himself, until a friend introduced him to self-compassion, and developing emotionally lose relationships with friends. As Vishwanath made space to nurture that vulnerability within himself, he became radically more comfortable expressing his feelings, setting boundaries and prioritizing rest when needed. He experienced life with more vibrant presence.

Research shows that people who actively nurture themselves enjoy a multitude of benefits, from less anxiety and depression to increased life satisfaction. A study found that 89% of those who practice self-care feel more motivated, confident and cheerful. Self-love deficiency has been linked to higher risks for addiction, suicide, violence and disordered eating behaviors. Nurturing yourself isn't just a nice-to-have, it's actually critical for mental health and overall human thriving.

At the end of the day, how you treat yourself sets the thermostat for how you move through the world. If you approach yourself with depletion, criticism, or neglect, that scarcity will shape your mindset and spirit. But on the other hand, nourishing your mind, body and soul helps rewire your operating system to one of inherent worthiness, abundance and tenderness with all of life.

So if you've been running on empty for too long, let this be your invitation to come back home to yourself. To rediscover the simple yet profound power of basic self-care. Of filling up your own cup first so that your glass isn't empty. Of treasuring this one sacred life you've been given by intentionally nurturing your whole self - mind, body, heart and spirit.

It's the most radical act of love, service and change-making you can offer this world. Because you simply cannot pour from an empty vessel. So take a deep breath and begin refilling yours, even just a little at a time.

**Nurturing oneself is a vital practice that involves caring for our physical, emotional, and spiritual well-being. Here's an explanation of 10 actionable items:**

1. Building a morning routine that starts your day gently can help you ease into the day with a sense of calm and mindfulness. Practices like meditation, journaling, visualization, affirmations or enjoying a quiet cup of tea can set the tone for a more centered and balanced day.

2. Blocking off self-care time windows in your calendar as non-negotiable appointments ensures that you prioritize your well-being amidst the demands of daily life. Treating self-care as a commitment can help you consistently dedicate time for nurturing activities.

3. Identifying physical practices that rejuvenate you, such as nature walks, painting, breathing can provide opportunities for relaxation and rejuvenation. These activities can help release tension, reduce stress, and promote overall physical and mental well-being.

4. Reconnecting with hobbies, creativity, and play can ignite joy and a sense of rest. Engaging in activities that bring you happiness and allow you to express yourself can be a form of self-nurturing and can provide a much-needed break from the demands of everyday life.

5. Keeping healthy snacks and beverages on hand for mindful nourishment throughout the day can help you

maintain energy levels and avoid the temptation of unhealthy choices. Mindful eating and hydration can contribute to overall physical and mental well-being.

6. Infusing your spaces with items that soothe your senses, such as art work, lighting, plants, cozy textiles, or uplifting quotes, can create a calming and nurturing environment. Surrounding yourself with elements that bring you comfort and joy can promote relaxation and a sense of peace.

7. Listening to your body's cues for rest and honoring its needs without resistance is crucial for self-nurturing. Allowing yourself to rest when needed, without guilt or self-judgment, can prevent burnout and promote overall well-being.

8. Tending to your inner child through imagination, childlike wonder, and unconditional nurturing can help you connect with your innate sense of playfulness and joy. Embracing your inner child can provide a sense of freedom and self-acceptance.

9. Setting boundaries around saying no and conserving your energy expenditure can help you avoid overcommitment and burnout. Learning to prioritize your needs and respecting your limits is an essential aspect of self-nurturing.

10. Building a self-nurturing support squad who can provide encouragement and accountability to help you stay motivated and committed to your self-care practices. Surrounding yourself with supportive individuals who understand the importance of self-nurturing can be invaluable.

**Here are 20 questions to assess if you are on the way to nurturing yourself, along with explanations:**

1. Do you make time for activities that bring you joy and relaxation? Engaging in activities that you genuinely enjoy and find relaxing is essential for self-nurturing. These can be hobbies, creative pursuits, or simply activities that allow you to unwind and disconnect from stress.

2. How often do you practice mindfulness or meditation? Mindfulness practices, such as meditation or deep breathing exercises, can help you cultivate a sense of presence and awareness, reducing stress and promoting emotional well-being. Regular practice can enhance your ability to stay grounded and focused.

3. Do you prioritize getting enough sleep and rest? Adequate sleep and rest are crucial for physical and mental rejuvenation. Neuroscience research has shown that sleep plays a vital role in memory consolidation, emotional regulation, and overall cognitive function.

4. When was the last time you engaged in physical activity that you enjoy? Regular physical activity can promote overall health and well-being. Engaging in physical activities that you genuinely enjoy, rather than perceiving them as a chore, can make the experience more nurturing and sustainable.

5. Do you make conscious efforts to nourish your body with nutrient-dense foods? Proper nutrition is essential for overall health and well-being. Mindful choices about what you consume can positively impact your energy levels, mood, and overall vitality.

6. How often do you spend time in nature or outdoors? Spending time in nature has been shown to have numerous benefits for mental and physical well-being. The natural environment can promote relaxation, reduce stress levels, and enhance overall mood and cognitive function.

7. Do you have a support system of friends or loved ones with whom you can share your thoughts and feelings? Having a supportive social network is crucial for emotional well-being. Sharing your thoughts and feelings with trusted individuals can provide a sense of connection and validation.

8. When was the last time you engaged in a creative or artistic activity? Creativity and artistic expression can be powerful forms of self-nurturing. Engaging in creative pursuits can promote self-expression, stress relief, and a sense of accomplishment.

9. Do you make time for personal growth and learning? Continuous learning and personal growth can contribute to a sense of fulfillment and self-nurturing.

Pursuing knowledge or skills that interest you can provide a sense of accomplishment and personal enrichment.

10. Do you practice self-compassion and kindness towards yourself? Self-compassion involves treating yourself with kindness, understanding, and acceptance, rather than harsh self-criticism. Neuroscience research has shown that self-compassion can reduce stress and improve emotional well-being.

11. How often do you take breaks from work or responsibilities? Taking regular breaks is essential for preventing burnout and maintaining a healthy work-life balance. Stepping away from responsibilities can provide mental rest and rejuvenation.

12. Do you have a relaxing bedtime routine? A calming bedtime routine can help prepare your mind and body for restful sleep. Practices like reading, taking a warm bath, or practicing gentle stretches can promote relaxation and better sleep quality.

13. Do you make time for activities that challenge you and stimulate your mind? Engaging in mentally stimulating activities can promote cognitive health and a sense of personal growth. This could include learning new skills, solving puzzles, or exploring new topics of interest.

14. When was the last time you expressed gratitude or appreciation for yourself? Practicing self-gratitude involves acknowledging and appreciating your own strengths, accomplishments, and positive qualities. This can foster a sense of self-worth and self-nurturing.

15. Do you set boundaries to protect your personal time and energy? Setting healthy boundaries is essential for self-nurturing. It involves learning to say no to commitments or demands that drain your energy or compromise your well-being.

16. Do you make time for solitude and quiet reflection? Solitude and quiet reflection can provide opportunities for introspection, self-awareness, and emotional processing. These moments of stillness can be incredibly nurturing for the mind and soul.

17. Do you have a safe and comfortable space dedicated to relaxation and self-care? Creating a dedicated space for self-care, whether it's a cozy corner or a relaxing room, can promote a sense of sanctuary and retreat from the demands of daily life.

18. Do you engage in activities that promote self-expression and emotional release? Finding healthy outlets for self-expression and emotional release, such as journaling, art, or physical exercise, can be nurturing for mental and emotional well-being.

19. Do you celebrate your achievements and successes, no matter how small? Acknowledging and celebrating your achievements, even the small ones, can foster a sense of self-appreciation and nurturing self-worth.

20. Do you make time for activities that promote self-discovery and personal growth? Engaging in activities that promote self-discovery and personal growth, such as exploring new interests, seeking personal therapy, or participating in self-development workshops, can contribute to a deeper understanding and nurturing of the self.

Nourishing and cherishing all of who you are isn't frivolous or selfish - it's an incredible offering to this world. A full cup lets you show up more vibrantly, wholeheartedly and passionately for all that you love.

# Neuroscience research Quoted in Chapter 5: Nurturing yourself

In today's fast-paced world, the importance of self-care is often overlooked. However, neuroscientific research increasingly demonstrates that nurturing ourselves is not just a luxury, but a necessity for optimal brain function and overall well-being.

1. The Neurological Basis of Self-Care

Recent studies in neuroscience have shed light on how self-care practices directly impact our brain structure and function. For instance, a study published in the journal "Biological Psychiatry" (Hölzel et al., 2011) found that mindfulness meditation practice leads to increases in regional brain gray matter density. This suggests that consistent self-care activities can actually change the physical structure of our brains.

2. Stress and the Brain

Chronic stress, often a result of neglecting self-care, has been shown to have detrimental effects on the brain. Research published in "Nature Neuroscience" (Arnsten, 2009) demonstrates that chronic stress can lead to atrophy in areas of the brain associated with executive function and self-regulation, particularly the prefrontal cortex. Conversely, engaging in stress-reducing activities as part of a self-care routine can help protect and even strengthen these crucial brain regions.

## 3. The Neuroscience of Sleep

Sleep is a critical component of self-care, and its importance is backed by extensive neuroscientific research. A study in the journal "Science" (Xie et al., 2013) revealed that sleep is crucial for clearing out neural waste products that accumulate during waking hours. This "brain cleaning" process is essential for maintaining cognitive function and overall brain health.

## 4. Exercise and Brain Health

Physical activity, another key aspect of self-care, has profound effects on brain health. A review in the journal "Trends in Cognitive Sciences" (Voss et al., 2013) summarized how exercise increases the production of new neurons (neurogenesis) in the hippocampus, a brain region crucial for learning and memory. Regular physical activity has also been linked to improved mood and reduced risk of neurodegenerative diseases.

## 5. Nutrition and Cognitive Function

The food we eat as part of our self-care routine directly impacts our brain function. Research published in "Nature Reviews Neuroscience" (Gómez-Pinilla, 2008) highlights how nutrients influence cognitive processes and neuroplasticity. For example, omega-3 fatty acids and flavonoids have been shown to support cognitive function and protect against brain aging.

## 6. Social Connection and Brain Health

Nurturing social connections is an often-overlooked aspect of self-care. However, neuroscience research emphasizes its importance. A study in the journal "Nature Neuroscience" (Eisenberger & Cole, 2012) found that social connection is associated with reduced inflammation in the body, which has protective effects on the brain.

## 7. Mindfulness and Emotional Regulation

Mindfulness practices, increasingly recognized as valuable self-care tools, have been shown to enhance emotional regulation. Research published in "Frontiers in Human Neuroscience" (Tang et al., 2015) demonstrates that mindfulness meditation can lead to increased activity in the prefrontal cortex and reduced activity in the amygdala, facilitating better emotional control.

## 8. Creativity and Cognitive Flexibility

Engaging in creative activities as part of self-care can enhance cognitive flexibility. A study in the journal "Creativity Research Journal" (Beaty et al., 2014) used fMRI to show that creative thinking activates a complex network of brain regions associated with cognitive control and spontaneous thought.

## 9. The Neuroscience of Gratitude

Practicing gratitude, a simple yet powerful self-care technique, has been shown to have measurable effects on the brain. Research published in "NeuroImage" (Kini et al., 2016) found that gratitude practice is associated with lasting changes in the medial prefrontal cortex, an area involved in learning and decision making.

## 10. Conclusion

Neuroscientific research clearly demonstrates that self-care practices have tangible, measurable effects on our brain structure and function. By engaging in regular self-care activities such as adequate sleep, exercise, mindfulness, and social connection, we can actively promote our brain health and overall well-being.

Remember, nurturing yourself isn't just about feeling good in the moment—it's about investing in the long-term health and resilience of your brain. As neuroscience continues to uncover the intricate ways in which our daily habits shape our brain function, the importance of consistent, mindful self-care becomes increasingly clear.

By understanding the neuroscience behind self-care, we can approach these practices not as indulgences, but as essential components of a brain-healthy lifestyle. In doing so, we set ourselves up for improved cognitive function, emotional regulation, and overall quality of life.

# Chapter 6
## Recognizing the inner voice

In a world that constantly bombards us with noise and outside voices insisting they know what's best, it's easy to get disconnected from our own inner compass. The subtle whispers of our intuition, our deepest callings, our truth - they get drowned out by the deafening roar of societal expectations, self-doubt, and loud illusions about how we're "supposed" to exist.

But here's what I've learned on this winding journey of life - recognizing and fiercely protecting our inner voice may just be one of the most radical, courageous and important acts of self-love and personal empowerment we'll ever take on. Because when we relearn how to tune into and trust those gut instincts, secret longings, and authentic needs arising from our soul, everything shifts.

Suddenly, we stop living according to fear-based narratives imposed by others. We stop abandoning ourselves to please, perform or chase empty metrics of success. Instead, we reclaim the spiritual birthright of authoring our own lives from a place of truth, integrity and self-trust. We remember that we are the ultimate authority and author of our stories.

I've witnessed this transformative process of reclaiming one's inner voice up close - and it's nothing short of a reclamation of personal power. Like with my friend Amar, who for years ignored the nagging feeling that his corporate career was slowly killing his spirit. He just kept trudging along out of obligation, telling himself he should be grateful, that his inner critic was the voice to listen to. Until one day, he hit a breaking point and was forced to go within. As Amar began meditating, soul-searching, and tenderly holding space for his deepest knowing to arise, he realized his inner voice had been urgently trying to wake him up to another path all along – of becoming a restaurateur - one of feeding his passions, living in alignment, and reclaiming his joy.

Then there's Jay, who grew up sacrificing his emotional needs in service of family and cultural pressures. Any time he felt small pangs of sadness or sensitivity, he'd hear his father's stern voice echoing to "toughen up". So Jay mastered the art of repressing his inner voice - that is, until his body and psyche started paying the price through burnout, anger issues and disconnection. In his later years, through a lot of self-reflection, support and therapy, he began the courageous work of feeling into his authentic needs and letting his true self speak up again after years of being silenced.

Research verifies how vital this work of heeding our inner voice is for wholeness and thriving. Dr. Shankar Vedantam's book "The Hidden Brain" reveals that from a neurological perspective, that gut instinct arises from a deep intelligence always weighing thousands of variables and trying to warn us when we're missing key pieces of information. Meanwhile, those who routinely ignore their intuition and authentic needs face increased risks of anxiety, depression, psychosomatic illnesses, and lives of quiet desperation.

At the most fundamental level, blocking our inner voice cuts us off from the essence of who we are - the part of us that craves purpose, fulfilment, intimacy and living in integrity with our values and callings. When we dismiss those inner nudges and urgings, we get stuck in a trance of deadening our aliveness. We betray our wholeness by abandoning the sacred information trying to arise from within.

So if you've been feeling a vague sense of unease, stuckness, longing, dissonance, perhaps that's your own inner voice trying to lovingly wake you up and guide you home to your truth. Maybe it's beckoning you away from the grind, or from a situation out of alignment. Maybe it's asking you to honor your worthiness, or shed self-limiting scripts, or simply embrace more magic and delight into your precious life.

No matter what form the whispers take, I invite you to listen. Turn inward and create intentional space to sit with the stirrings, knowing and emotions arising. Through quietude, curiosity, and an open heart, give yourself permission to finally hear the sacred song lines your soul has been trying to share all along. There is wisdom, light and an abiding source of guidance awaiting you there.

From this inner attunement, you'll unleash a power and wholeness that can't be matched. You reclaim your right to be the lead author of your story rather than a bystander in someone else's narrative. You regain access to the full force of your intuition and discernment. Most importantly, you start living in resonance with your authenticity, allowing your spirit to soar.

**10 actionable insights with practical examples:**

1. Carve out daily quiet time to simply listen - meditate, journal, take a silent walk and tune into yourself.

Example: Every morning, spend 15 minutes sitting in silence, focusing on your breath. Or, take a quiet walk in nature and observe your thoughts and feelings without judgment.

2. Start noticing the thoughts, feelings or body signals that arise when you're out of alignment - pay attention.

Example: When you feel tightness in your chest or a sense of unease, pause and reflect on what might be causing this misalignment with your true self.

3. Identify the external voices/programming that tend to drown out your inner knowing and set boundaries around them.

Example: If certain people or social media accounts make you doubt yourself, limit your exposure to them or mute notifications.

4. Explore heart-centered practices like breathwork, movement, time in nature to drop into your intuitive wisdom.

Example: Practice deep breathing exercises, go for a mindful walk in the park, or try gentle yoga to connect with your body and intuition.

5. Enlist a counselor or guide to help translate the messages arising within and unpack limiting beliefs.

Example: Work with a therapist or life coach who can help you identify and reframe negative self-talk or limiting beliefs that silence your inner voice.

6. Read works from authors/teachers who can attune you to your inner authority and worth.

Example: Read books or listen to podcasts by authors who encourage self-trust and self-acceptance, such as Brené Brown or Oprah Winfrey.

7. Make a list of all the times your intuition has divinely guided you; honor this source of intelligence.

Example: Reflect on times when you followed your gut instinct and it led to a positive outcome, and express gratitude for your intuition.

8. Notice when you're people-pleasing or abandoning yourself out of fear or obligation - pause and realign.

Example: If you find yourself saying "yes" to something you don't want to do, take a step back and check in with your true desires.

9. Visualize gathering all your scattered parts (your thoughts, fears, divergent opinions) back into wholeness, in integrity with your deepest truth.

Example: Imagine all the aspects of yourself coming together in harmony, aligning with your authentic self and highest values.

10. Spend time with others who are listening to and expressing their inner voice; let it inspire yours.

Example: Surround yourself with friends or mentors who are confident in their beliefs and true to themselves, letting their authenticity inspire you.

**Here are 20 questions to see if we are in touch with and recognizing our true inner voice:**

1. Do you often find yourself going along with decisions or situations that don't feel quite right, even if you can't pinpoint why?

If you tend to ignore your gut instincts or inner guidance, even when something feels off, it could be a sign that you're not fully connected to your inner voice. Our intuition often speaks to us in subtle ways, and learning to tune in to these signals is crucial for making choices that align with our deepest truth.

2. Do you frequently seek external validation or approval before trusting your own judgment?

Relying too heavily on others' opinions or seeking constant reassurance can be a sign that you're not fully trusting your inner wisdom. While it's healthy to consider different perspectives, ultimately you need to cultivate the confidence to follow your own guidance and trust your instincts.

3. Do you struggle with setting boundaries or saying "no" when you're overcommitted or stretched too thin?

If you have a hard time honoring your limits and prioritizing your needs, it could be a sign that you're not fully in touch with your inner voice. Listening to your intuition can help you discern when you're taking on too much and need to set boundaries.

4. Do you often make decisions based on what you "should" do or what others expect, rather than what feels truly right for you?

When we're disconnected from our inner voice, we can easily fall into the trap of living by external expectations or societal norms, rather than following our authentic path. Tuning in to your inner guidance can help you discern what truly resonates with you.

5. Do you frequently second-guess yourself or struggle with self-doubt, even when you've carefully considered a decision?

Chronic self-doubt or second-guessing can be a sign that you're not fully trusting your inner wisdom. Neuroscience research has shown that our gut instincts and intuition are often more accurate than we give them credit for, as they tap into the vast processing power of our unconscious mind.

6. Do you find yourself constantly seeking advice or input from others, even on decisions that primarily impact you?

While seeking advice can be helpful, an over-reliance on others' opinions can indicate that you're not fully connected to your own inner guidance system. Learning to trust your inner voice is key to making choices that truly resonate with your authentic self.

7. Do you often feel disconnected from your body or struggle to interpret its signals?

Our bodies are incredibly wise and can provide us with valuable intuitive cues when we're attuned to them. If you frequently ignore or override your body's messages, it could be a sign that you're not fully listening to your inner voice.

8. Do you find yourself frequently suppressing or ignoring your emotions, even when they're trying to communicate something important?

Our emotions are closely tied to our intuition and can provide us with valuable insights when we're willing to listen to them. If you tend to shut down or rationalize your feelings, you may be missing out on important guidance from your inner voice.

9. Do you often feel like you're "going through the motions" or living on autopilot, rather than feeling fully present and engaged in your life?

When we're disconnected from our inner voice, it's easy to fall into a state of numbness or dissociation, where we're simply going through the motions of life rather than living with intention and authenticity.

10. Do you struggle with making decisions or find yourself constantly second-guessing your choices, even after careful consideration?

Indecisiveness or chronic second-guessing can be a sign that you're not fully trusting your inner guidance system. Neuroscience research suggests that our intuition and unconscious mind can process vast amounts of information and provide us with accurate gut instincts, if we're willing to listen.

11. Do you often feel like you're living a life that's not truly your own, or that you're playing a role or meeting others' expectations rather than being your authentic self?

With the pace of external life and comparisons, it's easy to fall into patterns of people-pleasing or conforming to external expectations, rather than living a life that truly resonates with our deepest values and desires.

12. Do you tend to ignore or rationalize your intuitive hunches or gut feelings, even when they're persistent or strong?

Our intuition is a powerful source of guidance, and neuroscience research has shown that our gut instincts can tap into the vast processing power of our unconscious mind. If you consistently ignore or explain away these intuitive signals, you may be missing out on valuable insights.

13. Do you often find yourself feeling stuck or paralyzed when faced with important decisions, unable to access your inner knowing?

Our inner voice can whisper to us the clarity and guidance we need to make important choices. Learning to tune in to your intuition and trust your inner wisdom can help you move through periods of indecision with greater ease.

14. Do you frequently feel like you're carrying around a heavy burden or sense of inauthenticity, as if you're not living in alignment with your true self?

Inauthenticity, narcissism, imposter syndrome, mental health symptoms are a result of a sense of disconnection or dissonance within us, as if we're living a life that's not truly our own. Reconnecting with your authentic self and inner guidance can help alleviate this sense of burden or inauthenticity.

15. Do you struggle to access a sense of genuine joy, enthusiasm, or zest for life, even during periods when things are going well externally?

Our inner voice is the source of our deepest passion, aliveness, and appreciation for the present moment. If you frequently feel numb, apathetic, or disconnected from sincere enjoyment – even amid positive circumstances – it could indicate a lack of attunement to your inner guidance.

16. Do you struggle with making decisions that honor your deepest values or prioritize your well-being, even when you know what's best for you?

We find deep inner satisfaction when we live our life closely tied to our deepest values and sense of self-care. If you find yourself consistently making choices that go against your core values or neglect your well-being, it could be a sign that you're not fully listening to your inner guidance.

17. Do you often feel like you're living a life that's disconnected from your true purpose and meaning, as if a larger reason for existence is missing?

Being aligned with our authentic selves can provide us the fuel to live a life of purpose and meaning and strive to make a difference to other people's lives and to strive for the greater good.

18. Do you frequently find yourself caught up in negative self-talk or harsh inner criticism, drowning out the voice of self-compassion and kindness?

Neuroscience research suggests that self-criticism activates the same pathways in the brain as physical pain. If you struggle with a relentless inner critic, it may be a sign that you're not fully tapped into the nurturing, compassionate aspects of your inner voice.

19. Do you often feel like you're living a life dictated by fear, obligation, or external pressures, rather than following the path that feels most true and aligned for you?

Fear, obligation and external pressures can deplete us of vital life energy and we can fee drained and exhausted by getting swept up in societal expectations or a sense of duty - rather than honoring the path that feels most authentic to us. Tuning in to our inner guidance can help us navigate life from a place of truth and alignment.

20. Do you struggle to access a sense of inner peace, clarity, or groundedness, even when everything around you is relatively calm?

We can tap into the deep wisdom, clarity, and groundedness that is always available to us when we listen with self love. If you frequently feel unsettled, anxious, or ungrounded - even in moments of outer calm – it could be a sign that you're not fully connected to the still, centered aspects of your inner guidance.

By reflecting on these questions and noticing any areas where you may be disconnected from your inner voice, you can begin to cultivate a deeper relationship with your authentic self and live a life that feels more true, purposeful, and fulfilling.

# Neuroscience Research Quoted in Chapter 6: Recognizing the inner voice

## The Neuroscience of Inner Voice and Intuition: A Scientific Perspective

### Introduction

The concept of "inner voice" or intuition has long been a subject of interest in psychology and neuroscience. Recent advancements in neuroimaging and cognitive science have provided new insights into the neural mechanisms underlying intuitive decision-making and self-awareness. Here we explore the scientific understanding of our "inner voice" and its role in decision-making and personal well-being.

### Neural Basis of Intuition

Neuroscientific research has shed light on the brain processes involved in intuitive decision-making:

1. The Role of the Insula: The insula, a region of the cerebral cortex, plays a crucial role in interoception - the perception of internal bodily states. Critchley et al. (2004) found that activity in the insula is associated with awareness of visceral responses, which contributes to what we often call "gut feelings" [1].

2. Unconscious Information Processing: Bechara et al. (1997) demonstrated through the Iowa Gambling Task

that individuals can make advantageous decisions before conscious awareness of the strategy, suggesting a neural basis for intuition [2].

3. Default Mode Network (DMN): Research by Raichle et al. (2001) identified the DMN, a network of brain regions active during rest and self-referential thinking. This network is thought to play a role in introspection and accessing internal knowledge [3].

**Neuroscience of Self-Awareness and Inner Dialogue**

The concept of an "inner voice" is closely related to self-awareness and internal monologue:

1. Neural Correlates of Self-Reflection: Johnson et al. (2002) used fMRI to show that self-referential thinking activates specific regions in the medial prefrontal cortex, potentially forming the neural basis of our sense of self. [4]

2. Inner Speech and Language Areas: Geva et al. (2011) found that inner speech activates similar brain regions to external speech, including Broca's area and the left inferior frontal gyrus, suggesting a neurological basis for our internal dialogue [5].

**Intuition in Decision-Making**

Scientific studies have explored the role of intuition in decision-making processes:

1. Dual-Process Theory: Kahneman's (2011) work on fast and slow thinking suggests that intuition (System 1) operates quickly and automatically, while analytical thinking (System 2) is slower and more deliberate [6].

2. Expertise and Intuition: Klein's (1998) research on naturalistic decision-making showed that experts often rely on intuition based on pattern recognition, which is rooted in extensive experience [7].

**Neurobiology of Emotional Intelligence**

Emotional intelligence, often associated with intuition, has been studied from a neuroscientific perspective:

1. Amygdala and Emotional Processing: LeDoux's (1996) work on the amygdala highlighted its role in emotional processing and its influence on decision-making [8].

2. Prefrontal Cortex in Emotion Regulation: Davidson et al. (2000) demonstrated the prefrontal cortex's involvement in regulating emotional responses, a key aspect of emotional intelligence [9].

**Mindfulness and Brain Plasticity**

Practices aimed at enhancing self-awareness and intuition have been shown to affect brain structure and function:

1. Meditation and Brain Changes: Lazar et al. (2005) found that long-term meditation practice is associated with increased cortical thickness in brain regions related to attention and sensory processing [10].

2. Neuroplasticity and Mental Training: Davidson and Lutz (2008) reviewed evidence suggesting that mental training through meditation can alter brain function and structure, potentially enhancing intuitive capabilities [11].

## Conclusion

While the concept of an "inner voice" may seem abstract, neuroscientific research provides evidence for the neural mechanisms underlying intuition, self-awareness, and internal dialogue. Understanding these processes can help individuals make more informed decisions and potentially enhance their ability to tap into their intuitive capabilities.

However, it's important to note that while intuition can be valuable, it should be balanced with analytical thinking, especially in complex decision-making scenarios. Future research may provide even more insights into how we can effectively integrate intuitive and analytical processes for optimal decision-making and personal growth.

# References

[1] Critchley, H. D., et al. (2004). Neural systems supporting interoceptive awareness. Nature Neuroscience, 7(2), 189-195.

[2] Bechara, A., et al. (1997). Deciding advantageously before knowing the advantageous strategy. Science, 275(5304), 1293-1295.

[3] Raichle, M. E., et al. (2001). A default mode of brain function. Proceedings of the National Academy of Sciences, 98(2), 676-682.

[4] Johnson, S. C., et al. (2002). Neural correlates of self-reflection. Brain, 125(8), 1808-1814.

[5] Geva, S., et al. (2011). The neural correlates of inner speech defined by voxel-based lesion-symptom mapping. Brain, 134(10), 3071-3082.

[6] Kahneman, D. (2011). Thinking, fast and slow. Farrar, Straus and Giroux.

[7] Klein, G. (1998). Sources of power: How people make decisions. MIT Press.

[8] LeDoux, J. E. (1996). The emotional brain: The mysterious underpinnings of emotional life. Simon & Schuster.

[9] Davidson, R. J., et al. (2000). Dysfunction in the neural circuitry of emotion regulation--a possible prelude to violence. Science, 289(5479), 591-594.

[10] Lazar, S. W., et al. (2005). Meditation experience is associated with increased cortical thickness. Neuroreport, 16(17), 1893-1897.

[11] Davidson, R. J., & Lutz, A. (2008). Buddha's brain: Neuroplasticity and meditation. IEEE Signal Processing Magazine, 25(1), 176-174.

# Chapter 7
# The power of prayer

In a world that can often feel fraught with chaos, division and upheaval, many of us long for access to a deeper source of peace, refuge and reassurance. An anchor to steady us when the storms of life rage. A soft place to land with our heaviest burdens. A sanctuary where we can turn over our fears, doubts and deepest yearnings to something greater than ourselves.

For countless millions across cultures and traditions, that sanctuary has long been the power of prayer - a space of stillness, communion and openness to the sacred. A way of plugging into a higher frequency beyond the material realm. An invitation to surrender our limiting beliefs and finite willpower over to vast, more benevolent forces of love.

The word "prayer" can feel loaded and complex for some. But at its core, I've come to understand prayer as nothing more than the most intimate form of conversation with that which we deem sacred, divine or transcendent. Which for you may look like pleading with the Universe, sending love to your higher power, or simply taking refuge in the spaciousness of the present moment between thoughts.

No matter your beliefs, the healing, centering force available to us through prayer is undeniable and transformative when we let ourselves experience it. I've seen this firsthand through challenges that previously felt unbearable until I was able to hand them over to a greater power. Like when trauma from my past threatened to swallow me in fear and darkness until I started a practice of breathing deeply and inviting in light through simple prayerful mantras. Little by little, I felt tangible burdens lift as divine presence infused me with perspective and calm resilience.

Or the sustained sense of comfort and reassurance that comes from staying connected to that silent source of peace within - an unshakeable knowingness that we are being lovingly upheld, even when circumstances feel overwhelming or senseless. I remember watching a dear friend lose her young son to cancer... yet from the depths of her paralyzing grief, somehow she could still find the strength to carry on, access profound solace and abiding trust through her steadfast prayer life.

So many have found their unwavering prayers answered in ways that feel nothing short of miraculous. While more research is needed to fully understand the underlying mechanisms and the extent of these effects across different populations and contexts, here are some examples of the potential benefits of prayer based on neuroscience research:

1. Enhanced Focus and Attention: Studies have shown that prayer and meditation can activate the prefrontal cortex, which is responsible for focused attention and cognitive control. Researchers have observed increased activity in this brain region during prayer, suggesting that it may help individuals maintain a state of heightened focus and concentration.

2. Reduced Stress and Anxiety: Prayer has been associated with a decrease in the activity of the amygdala, the brain's fear center. When individuals engage in prayer, the amygdala shows reduced reactivity, leading to a calming effect and a potential reduction in stress and anxiety levels. This may be due to the sense of comfort and reassurance that prayer can provide.

3. Increased Emotional Regulation: Neuroscience research has found that prayer can influence the activity of the anterior cingulate cortex (ACC), a region involved in emotional regulation and conflict monitoring. During prayer, the ACC exhibits heightened activity, suggesting that prayer may enhance an individual's ability to regulate their emotions and manage conflicting thoughts or feelings.

These findings suggest potential benefits of prayer on brain function and emotional well-being. The stories of healing through prayer are supported by a wealth of scientific research showing its measurable physiological and psychological effects. Dr. Larry Dossey authored numerous books citing data that sustained prayer can improve immune functioning, accelerate recovery times, reduce anxiety and produce significant positive biochemical changes. Other peer-reviewed studies show prayer and mindfulness practices changing brain patterns to slow the buildup of neurofibril proteins implicated in Alzheimer's and dementia.

It's not just about individual healing or material gains. Prayer also has the power to benefit humanity on a mass scale by unleashing states of heightened love, compassion and social harmony. Research at John Templeton Foundation found the largest gatherings of group prayer and meditation measurably lowered violence, crime rates, warfare and civil unrest within a 300-mile radius of where they were held. The unified intention and concentration of these spiritual forces created distinct shifts on a collective level.

At the essence of all prayer is a profound surrendering of our finite sense of control, willpower and separateness over to something greater than ourselves as individuals. Which has incredible transformative power to move us out of our limited mental loops, stress cycles and fearful reactivity into the expansive presence of here and now. When we stop clinging so tightly to our attachments, resistances and obsessive need to figure everything out, the sacred space of prayer opens us to receive grace, blessings and guidance in ways we couldn't have orchestrated on our own.

This is the beauty and gift available to us all through prayer: A tangible way to center into the eternal peace always available beyond the circumstances of our ego and personality. A path to liberation through relinquishing the futile need to control everything through sheer force of human will. A conduit to tap into unconditional love, divine intelligence and unlimited potentials - if we're simply willing to let go and be guided.

So whether you're someone deeply steeped in ritual prayer through your religious traditions, or you consider tuning into the stillness of each present moment as your sacred conversation, give yourself over to it fully. Allow it to be the soft place you come home to. The sanctuary that helps you find clarity and rest in the midst of life's turbulence.

For each of us who drops our concrete attachments and willingness to fight reality as is, there is an infinite source of calm reassurance, grace and refuge available through prayer. All you have to do is slow down, turn inward and surrender into its loving embrace.

**10 actionable insights on experiencing the power of prayer:**

1. Having a daily ritual, like setting aside 10 minutes each morning for silent meditation or reading inspiring prayers, can anchor the day in peace and spiritual connection.

2. Before praying, taking a few deep breaths or doing a body scan can quiet the mind's busyness and allow you to be fully present, like hitting the reset button.

3. Making a list of specific prayer intentions, whether for yourself or others, gives clarity and focus rather than vague requests. Then let go of attachments.

4. Setting a timer for 5-20 minutes of pure stillness, without an agenda, can open you up to experiencing the sacred and receiving intuitive guidance.

5. Pausing to say a simple gratitude prayer when you see a beautiful sunset or finish a meal can enhance your appreciation for life's gifts.

6. Visualizing yourself releasing heavy burdens during prayer can be profoundly uplifting, like taking a weight off your shoulders and giving it to a higher power.

7. Prayer can be a dialogue - pour out your heart, but also stay attuned for any insights or nudges from within that may arise as intuitive guidance.

8. Praying collectively, whether with family or a group, creates a palpable energy and amplification from syncing up your intentions and vibrations.

9. The grandeur of nature can inspire wonder and reverence. Allowing it to elicit spontaneous prayers or expressions of wonder connect you to the divine.

10. Recording prayer intentions, experiences, and potential "answers" in a journal lets you track your spiritual journey and growth over time.

**Here are 20 questions on understanding and practicing the power of prayer:**

1. What traditions, religions, or spiritual practices did you grow up with that involved prayer? How did that shape your current views?

Our upbringing and exposure to religious/spiritual traditions shape our views on prayer from a young age. Exploring this background provides insight into our core beliefs and any assumptions we may be operating under.

2. Have you ever experienced what felt like an answered prayer or spiritual intervention? If so, what happened and how did it impact you?

Recounting personal experiences of prayers seemingly being "answered" or intuitive guidance arriving after prayer reinforces one's faith. Neuroscience shows the brain's reticular activating system filters perceptions based on where we focus attention.

3. What do you feel is the purpose or value of prayer? For example, is it connection, releasing burdens, manifesting desires, or something else?

Clarifying the purpose of prayer, whether for connection, burden relief, manifesting desires, etc. helps refine one's intentions and approach. Studies show focused spiritual prayer activates the brain's frontal lobe regions associated with focus/intention.

4. Do you ever experience resistance, doubts or struggle to prioritize prayer/meditation time? Why do you think that is?

Being honest about any resistances to consistently prioritizing prayer/meditation raises self-awareness about hurdles. The pre-frontal cortex's executive functions include motivation and regulating impulses.

5. What specific prayer practices or techniques have you found most meaningful or effective?

Sharing techniques like breathwork, chanting, visualization that have proven most effective for oneself provides wisdom to others. Rituals engage procedural memory encoding in the brain.

6. In what ways have you seen prayer impact your inner state - emotions, thoughts, sense of peace?

Noticing how prayer impacts inner states like emotions, mind-quieting and a sense of peace is part of the growth process. Meditation can de-activate the amygdala which processes anxiety/stress.

7. How might a consistent prayer practice support other areas of your life - work, relationships, health?

Exploring how a spiritual practice supports other life areas like work, relationships and health promotes an integrated wholeness approach. The brain inevitably links associated neural networks.

8. Have you explored different types of prayer like spoken word, silent meditation, movement, music?

Introducing variety like silent, spoken, movement, or musical prayer can re-engage the brain's novelty sensors to prevent staleness. Novel inputs spur dopamine release.

9. What stories from spiritual texts, teachings or lives of saints have inspired your beliefs about prayer?

Drawing inspiration from sacred stories, texts and lives of saints provides touchstones to evolve one's conception of prayer's significance. Narratives potentially encode new associative networks.

10. How have your beliefs or relationship to prayer evolved over time?

Examining how one's relationship to prayer has evolved over time lends a longitudinal perspective on the progression of faith and practice. As beliefs, practices and experiences with prayer change, the brain can reorganize its neural connections accordingly to integrate these new patterns. The brain remains continually evolves and is not fixed.

11. Neuroscience shows meditation can induce changes in brain regions associated with perception, cognition and emotion regulation. Can you relate to this based on your experience of prayer?

Research in neuroscience has found that the practice of meditation can actually change and affect certain regions of the brain. Specifically, it impacts areas like the insula, putamen, and prefrontal cortices. The insula is involved in self-awareness and emotional experience. The putamen plays a role in perception and learning from experiences. The prefrontal cortex is crucial for regulating emotions, making decisions, and focusing attention. When people meditate regularly, these brain regions can undergo functional and structural changes. The effects of meditation, like increased self-awareness, regulated emotions, and improved perception, may potentially overlap with the subjective experiences people report from prayer.

12. Do you ever experience your ego, fears, or negative self-talk arising as obstacles during prayer? Some teachings assert these must be transcended to experience true communion. What are your thoughts?

Being self-aware of when the ego, fears or negative self-talk arise as obstacles during prayer is key, as some teachings assert transcending these leads to deeper union.

The default mode network refers to a set of brain regions that are active when our minds are wandering or getting caught up in self-referential thoughts, like daydreaming or getting stuck in loops of worry. When the default mode network is very active, it's difficult for us to be fully present and aware of the current moment.

For true communion or deep spiritual connection during prayer, the default mode network needs to deactivate or quiet down. In other words, we need to disengage from that normal state of getting trapped in our own thoughts and inner chatter. Deactivating the default mode allows us to transcend our ego and self-focus, and instead be fully immersed in the experience of prayer and connection to something greater than ourselves.

We have to find a way to silence the constant background noise of our minds during prayer in order to experience it in a truly profound way.

13. How do you balance the paradox of praying for specific outcomes while also surrendering attachment and ego desires?

Finding the balance between praying for desired outcomes while surrendering control and attachments is an integral part of the spiritual path's paradoxes.

Our brains are wired with interconnected networks of neurons that are associated with different concepts, thoughts, and expectations we have. When we pray for specific outcomes or desires, certain neural networks related to those expected results get activated.

In order to find the right balance between praying for what we want while also surrendering control, we need to regulate or manage the neural networks associated with our expectations.

In simpler terms, we have to find a way to calm down the fired up brain circuits related to strongly desiring or grasping at particular outcomes from our prayers. Overactive expectations can conflict with the idea of surrendering attachment.

So we must create a balanced state in our minds - having clarity in our intentions when praying, but not getting hijacked by excessive longing or expectations hard-wired into our brain networks. Regulating those expectation networks allows for the surrender aspect of prayer.

14. Have you found power in praying for others, sending energy/wishes to specific people or global events?

Praying compassionately for others and global events can induce feelings of belonging to something greater.

The brain has specific circuits or networks of neurons that are associated with feelings of care, empathy, and connection to others, especially loved ones/family. These are referred to as the "care/kin circuits."

When we pray compassionately for others or send positive energy to people and events around the world, it can activate those care/kin circuits in our brains. It taps into the neural networks related to our natural inclination to care for others.

At the same time, praying for people beyond just our immediate circles helps "dissolve separateness." In simpler terms, it breaks down the mental barriers and distinctions we often maintain between ourselves and the rest of humanity or the world at large.

So by engaging in this type of compassionate prayer, we stimulate the brain's wiring for care and connection, while simultaneously removing our sense of being a separate, isolated individual. It creates a neural experience of oneness and integration with others and the larger universe.

15. In what ways does being in nature, observing beauty or syncing with natural rhythms enhance your prayer experience?

Nature's rhythms, beauty and grandeur can significantly enhance one's prayer experience by reducing mental chatter. Exposure to natural scenes induces a wakeful but relaxed brain state.

16. Prayer and meditation are often said to quiet the default mode network (explained earlier) of the brain associated with self-referential thoughts. How might a stillness facilitate spiritual awareness?

Prayer and meditation are thought to quiet the default mode network associated with self-referential, wandering thoughts, potentially opening portals to spiritual awareness by transcending the ego.

17. When is prayer most beneficial or necessary for you - in times of joy, struggle, uncertainty, grief?

Considering when prayer feels most beneficial and necessary - joy, struggle, uncertainty, grief - helps tailor one's approach for that season of life. The brain encodes associations – it creates and stores linked connections between different pieces of information, experiences, or concepts.

18. What is your experience explaining prayer's role to friends/family who don't share those spiritual beliefs?

Thoughtfully bridging one's spiritual view of prayer's role with friends/family requires navigating worldview gaps with care to avoid alienation or conflict.

19. How might developing a more disciplined, consistent practice over time elevate your experience of prayer's impact?

Consistently maintaining a disciplined and regular practice of prayer over an extended period of time can lead to experiencing prayer in a more profound and unified way. When prayer becomes an unwavering habit and routine, it allows the effects to become more integrated within your whole brain and being. Steadiness in your practice breeds a sort of harmonization, where the neural pathways, thought patterns, and physiological responses related to the experience of prayer become smoothly coordinated and ingrained. This integration creates a depth of experience and sense of union, where prayer feels like a seamless part of your overall state of consciousness and existence, rather than just an isolated activity.

20. Ultimately, do you view prayer as something you "do" or as a state of consciousness to embody?

Framing prayer as an embodied state of consciousness rather than merely a practice reveals the depths of one's belief that it's a way of being, not just doing.

The metaphors or analogies we use when describing something like prayer can reveal the underlying concepts and frameworks we have about it in our minds. The metaphorical language we choose exposes the core models or ways of thinking about prayer that are foundational to our beliefs and understandings.

For example, if someone refers to prayer as "a conversation with God", it shows their conceptual model is viewing prayer as a dialogue or personal interaction. But if they call it "tapping into a universal energy", it indicates their core concept frames prayer as connecting to a more impersonal force. The specific metaphor someone uses gives a window into the basic, guiding ideas structuring their conception of what prayer essentially is.

So in simple terms - the metaphors we use let us see the core, foundational models for how we conceptualize and make sense of abstract concepts like prayer in our minds.

Prayer is simply an invitation to move beyond the limits of your personal will and into cosmic realms where all things are endlessly worked for good. Let it be your refuge, your reassurance, your guide into higher Love.

**List of Neuroscience Research Quoted in Chapter 7: The power of prayer**

1. Prayer and meditation can activate the prefrontal cortex, which is responsible for focused attention and cognitive control.

2. Prayer has been associated with a decrease in the activity of the amygdala, the brain's fear center, potentially reducing stress and anxiety levels.

3. Prayer can influence the activity of the anterior cingulate cortex (ACC), a region involved in emotional regulation and conflict monitoring.

4. Studies show prayer and mindfulness practices can change brain patterns to slow the buildup of neurofibril proteins implicated in Alzheimer's and dementia.

5. The brain's reticular activating system filters perceptions based on where we focus attention, which may relate to experiences of "answered" prayers.

6. Focused spiritual prayer activates the brain's frontal lobe regions associated with focus and intention.

7. The pre-frontal cortex's executive functions include motivation and regulating impulses, which may be relevant to overcoming resistance to prayer practices.

8. Rituals engage procedural memory encoding in the brain.

9. Meditation can de-activate the amygdala, which processes anxiety and stress.

10. Novel inputs, such as varying prayer methods, can spur dopamine release in the brain.

11. As beliefs and practices with prayer change, the brain can reorganize its neural connections to integrate these new patterns.

12. Meditation can induce changes in brain regions associated with perception, cognition, and emotion regulation, specifically mentioning the insula, putamen, and prefrontal cortices.

13. The default mode network, a set of brain regions active during mind-wandering and self-referential thoughts, needs to deactivate for deeper spiritual connection during prayer.

14. Prayer can activate neural networks related to care and empathy, referred to as "care/kin circuits."

15. Exposure to natural scenes induces a wakeful but relaxed brain state, which can enhance prayer experiences.

16. The brain encodes associations between different pieces of information, experiences, or concepts, which is relevant to when prayer feels most beneficial.

17. Consistent prayer practice can lead to integration of neural pathways, thought patterns, and physiological responses related to the experience of prayer.

# Chapter 8
# Celebrating heartful joy

**Heartful Joy: The Essence of a Positive Life**

Joy is a profound and infectious emotion that radiates from within, illuminating our world with warmth and positivity. It is the spontaneous overflow of heartfelt contentment, an inner state of being that transcends fleeting moments of happiness. Heartful joy is a choice, a conscious decision to embrace the present with an open heart and a grateful mind.

**The Power of the Present Moment**

True joy resides in the present moment, for it is in the here and now that we can fully experience the beauty and wonder of life. When we immerse ourselves in the present, free from the burdens of the past or the anxieties of the future, we open ourselves to the pure essence of joy. Consider the simple act of savoring a delicious meal, the flavors dancing on your taste buds, the aroma filling your senses – in that moment, there is nothing but pure, unadulterated joy.

**Optimism: The Fuel for Joy**

Neuroscience has revealed the profound impact of optimism on our well-being and success. Optimistic individuals tend to live longer, healthier lives, experience lower levels of stress, and achieve greater success in their personal and professional endeavors. The reason? Optimism is a powerful force that shapes our perception, enabling us to see opportunities where others may see obstacles.

**Case Study: Radha's Optimistic Journey**

Radha was a young woman faced with a daunting challenge – a life-threatening illness that threatened to derail her dreams. Yet, instead of succumbing to despair, she chose to embrace optimism and heartful joy. With each treatment session, she focused on the progress she had made, the small victories that brought her closer to healing. She surrounded herself with loved ones who nurtured her spirit and celebrated every triumph, no matter how seemingly insignificant. Through her unwavering optimism, Radha not only conquered her illness but emerged stronger and more resilient, with a renewed appreciation for the beauty of life.

**Celebrating Heartful Joy: 10 Actionable Steps**

1. Practice Gratitude: Cultivate a daily habit of expressing gratitude for the blessings in your life, no matter how small. Write them down, share them with loved ones, or simply reflect on them in moments of stillness.

2. Embrace Mindfulness: Engage in mindfulness practices, such as meditation, deep breathing, or simply being present in the moment. This will help you connect with the here and now, allowing joy to flourish.

3. Surround Yourself with Positive People: Seek out individuals who radiate positivity and uplift your spirit. Their energy and enthusiasm can be contagious, fueling your own joy.

4. Find Moments of Wonder: Appreciate the beauty in the world around you, from the intricate patterns of nature to the intricate creations of humanity. Allowing yourself to be awed by the wonders of life can ignite heartful joy.

5. Engage in Joyful Activities: Pursue hobbies, interests, and activities that bring you genuine joy. Whether it's dancing, painting, gardening, or playing a sport, immerse yourself in experiences that fill your heart with happiness.

6. Spread Kindness: Acts of kindness, no matter how small, can have a profound impact on both the giver and the recipient. Share a sincere compliment, lend a helping hand, or simply offer a warm smile – these small gestures can cultivate heartful joy.

7. Embrace Challenges with Optimism: When faced with obstacles or setbacks, consciously choose to view them as opportunities for growth and learning. Approach challenges with a positive mindset, and you'll be better equipped to navigate them with resilience and grace.

8. Celebrate Small Victories: Recognize and celebrate the small wins and milestones in your life. These moments of achievement, no matter how seemingly insignificant, can fuel your sense of accomplishment and joy.

9. Nurture Meaningful Connections: Invest time and energy into building and maintaining meaningful relationships with loved ones. Shared experiences, laughter, and support can cultivate heartful joy and enrich your life.

10. Practice Self-Compassion: Be kind and gentle with yourself. Embrace your imperfections, forgive yourself for mistakes, and treat yourself with the same compassion you would extend to a dear friend. Self-compassion cultivates inner peace and joy.

## 20 Questions for celebrating heartful joy

1. Am I living in the present moment, or am I allowing past regrets or future anxieties to cloud my joy?

Instead of being fully engaged with your child playing at the park, you find yourself ruminating over a mistake you made at work yesterday or worrying about an upcoming deadline. You miss out on the pure joy of that present moment. Make a conscious effort to let go of the past and future and be fully present.

2. Do I actively cultivate an optimistic mindset, or do I tend to focus on the negative aspects of situations?

When you get passed over for a promotion, do you catastrophize and think you'll never get ahead? Or do you view it as a temporary setback and an opportunity to refocus your efforts? Optimistic self-talk like "This is a challenge I can overcome" fosters heartful joy.

3. How often do I express gratitude for the blessings in my life, both big and small?

Do you take time each day to appreciate things like your morning coffee, a sunny day, or a kind gesture from a stranger? Or do you largely take the positive for granted? Actively noting gratitude primes your mind for heartful joy.

4. Do I make time for mindfulness practices that help me connect with the present moment?

Simple acts like taking a few deep breaths, going for a mindful walk, or doing a body scan meditation help anchor you in the here-and-now where real joy lives. If you're constantly stuck in your head, make mindfulness a priority.

5. Am I surrounding myself with positive, uplifting individuals who fuel my heartful joy?

The friends who always complain and see the glass as half-empty can be draining over time. Prioritize relationships with those who live with an attitude of gratitude and see possibilities rather than limitations.

6. Do I intentionally seek out moments of wonder and awe in my daily life?

Did you pause to really take in the striking sunset on your drive home? Or did you just rush by that moment of beauty? Looking for awe-inspiring moments in nature or art cultivates heartful joy.

7. How often do I engage in activities or hobbies that genuinely bring me joy?

When's the last time you lost yourself in something you truly love, like playing your guitar, tending your garden, or reading a great novel? Don't let those soul-nurturing activities fall by the wayside.

8. Do I make a conscious effort to spread kindness and positivity to those around me?

Did you hold the door for someone or offer a genuine compliment today? Acts of kindness don't just brighten someone else's day - they awaken your own heartful joy.

9. When faced with challenges or setbacks, do I approach them with an optimistic mindset, seeing opportunities for growth?

If you failed an important exam, did you beat yourself up and assume you're just not smart enough? Or did you view it as an opportunity to study more effectively and grow from the experience?

10. Do I celebrate and acknowledge my small victories and achievements?

Did you take a moment to feel proud after finally getting your budget organized or learning a new recipe? Don't just move on to the next thing - pause and let yourself feel that moment of satisfaction.

11. Am I investing time and energy into nurturing meaningful connections with loved ones?

When you get home from work, do you truly connect with your family or just sit in front of the TV? Quality time deepens bonds and opens your heart to joy.

12. Do I practice self-compassion, treating myself with kindness and understanding?

Instead of beating yourself up over a mistake, did you show yourself the same compassion you'd give a dear friend? Self-compassion reduces negative self-talk that smothers heartful joy.

13. How often do I allow myself to experience heartful joy, free from feelings of guilt or self-judgment?

Did you turn down an invitation because you felt you "shouldn't" have fun until all your work was done? Don't deprive yourself of joy because of unrealistic expectations.

14. Am I actively working towards goals and aspirations that align with my purpose and values?

Are you just drifting through life, or are you taking steps daily toward hopes and dreams that give you a sense of meaning? Purposeful living opens the door to heartful joy.

15. Do I make time for self-reflection and personal growth, or am I stuck in patterns and routines?

When was the last time you evaluated whether your habits and mindsets are serving you? Self-reflection allows for positive change and personal evolution.

16. How do I respond to adversity – with resilience and optimism or with despair and negativity?

When you encountered a major life stressor like job loss or illness, did you cope by problem-solving and looking for silver linings? Or did you become overwhelmed by negativity?

17. Do I actively seek out opportunities to learn and expand my horizons, fueling my joy and personal growth?

Did you sign up for that cooking class or read a book on a new topic that fascinated you? Lifelong learning awakens wonder and joy.

18. Am I living a life that is true to my authentic self, or am I conforming to societal expectations at the expense of my joy?

Are you doing work you're passionate about and surrounding yourself with people/environments that energize you? Or do you try to fit an unhappy mold?

19. Do I make time for rest, relaxation, and self-care, or am I constantly pushing myself to the point of burnout?

Did you take time for a shower, a nature walk, or just putting your feet up today? Ignoring needs for renewal and replenishment ultimately zaps your joy.

20. Am I actively cultivating heartful joy in my life, or am I allowing external circumstances to dictate my emotional state?

Are you making conscious choices like gratitude, mindfulness, and optimism to nurture heartful joy daily? Or do you let moods and situations overrule your ability to find joy?

By regularly reflecting on these questions, we can assess our progress in celebrating heartful joy and make adjustments as needed to align our lives with this profound and transformative state of being.

**Neuroscience related topics quoted in Chapter 8: Celebrating heartful joy**

1. Optimism: Neuroscience research suggests that optimism is associated with increased activation in the rostral anterior cingulate cortex and amygdala, areas involved in emotional regulation and processing positive information.

2. Joy and positive emotions: Studies show that positive emotions activate the brain's reward centers, particularly the ventral striatum and the ventromedial prefrontal cortex, releasing neurotransmitters like dopamine and serotonin.

3. Mindfulness: Neuroimaging studies indicate that regular mindfulness practice can lead to increased gray matter density in brain regions associated with learning, memory, emotion regulation, and perspective taking.

4. Gratitude: Expressing gratitude has been linked to increased activity in the medial prefrontal cortex, an area associated with learning and decision making.

5. Present moment awareness: Research suggests that being present activates the insula, a region involved in bodily awareness and integration of sensory information.

6. Social connections: Neuroscience shows that positive social interactions trigger the release of oxytocin, often

called the "bonding hormone," which can reduce stress and increase trust and empathy.

7. Kindness and altruism: Acts of kindness activate the brain's pleasure centers, releasing endorphins and creating a "helper's high."

8. Resilience: Studies indicate that resilience is associated with increased connectivity between the prefrontal cortex and the amygdala, allowing for better emotional regulation in stressful situations.

9. Self-compassion: Neuroimaging studies suggest that self-compassion activates the care-giving system in the brain, associated with feelings of safety and security.

10. Goal-setting and motivation: The brain's reward system, particularly the ventral striatum, is activated when we anticipate achieving goals, promoting motivation.

11. Habits and routines: Neuroscience shows that habits are formed in the basal ganglia, and as behaviors become more automatic, brain activity shifts from the prefrontal cortex to this region.

12. Learning and neuroplasticity: Research demonstrates that learning new skills can lead to structural changes in the brain, with increased gray matter in areas relevant to the skill being learned.

13. Rest and relaxation: Studies show that rest and relaxation activate the parasympathetic nervous system and default mode network in the brain, essential for cognitive function and creativity.

14. Authenticity: While less directly studied, being authentic is associated with reduced activity in brain regions linked to conflict and anxiety, suggesting less internal struggle.

15. Decision-making: Neuroscience research indicates that decision-making involves complex interactions between emotional (limbic system) and rational (prefrontal cortex) brain areas.

# Chapter 9
## Deepest gratitude

Can you feel that gentle pulse of life within you? The rhythm of life itself, flowing through your veins? What an incredible gift we've been given - human forms to experience the full spectrum of existence.

Too often, we let the busyness of daily life numb us. We rush past the profound miracle of simply being able to sip a warm cup of tea, feel the caress of a spring breeze, hear the laughter of a loved one. We take for granted abilities like breathing easily, moving our bodies, tasting the sweetness of a ripe strawberry.

But what if we slowed down and let ourselves be blown away by it all? What if we opened our senses to truly witness the intricate choreography of biodiversity unfolding around us? Allowed ourselves to be left in humble awe by the cosmic improbability that any of this exists at all?

By choosing to express deep, overflowing gratitude for the smallest things, we unlock the ability to experience the richness of every blessed moment. No longer do we miss the sheer magic constantly dancing for our attention in each sight, smell, texture and thrum of aliveness.

I've glimpsed this expansive state of appreciation, and I can tell you - it's one of the purest highs and most direct pathways to inhabiting our soul's brightest light. Like that morning years ago, when I woke up after a night of dreamy visions feeling so stunningly grateful just to be alive. As I lay there bathing in the soft newness of dawn's first rays, I experienced the profound gift of being able to breathe, to feel my heart steadily beating within my chest. Every minuscule rustle and birdsong outside felt sacrosanct and purposeful, offering itself up as a humble celebration simply for the miracle of consciousness witnessing it.

In those transcendent instances, the boundaries between our mind, body and soul dissolve as we steep in supreme nourishment from the inexhaustible wellspring of existence itself. We shed our layers of heaviness to drink directly from the source. We awaken to the revelation that our very presence is woven from the same luminous essence and cosmic genius as every other "thing" perceived through our peripatetic senses.

The latest neuroscience backs up what the ancients have long understood - that cultivating sincere gratitude quite literally alters our being at a neural level to counteract aging, anxiety and disease. MRI studies show gratitude practices produce powerful effects, including increased dopamine and serotonin production while activating the brain's bliss biosystem and reducing cortisol levels. Thoughts and sensations of gratefulness quite tangibly influence our neurochemistry in nourishing ways.

More than just individual benefits, expressing deep gratitude can also beneficially reshape our communities and our world. By centering our awareness first from a space of abundance rather than lack or fear, we realign our personal energies in a way that naturally inspires more connection, generosity and flow around us. We become catalysts for making positive systemic changes as we embody the solutions we wish to see most.

Just look at the some of the indigenous tribes of Brazil's Amazon rainforest who deliberately start every day with a group gratitude practice of chanting and breathwork. By attuning together to revere the generosity of nature, this helps foster a ubiquitous mindset of sustainable stewardship passed down over generations. Their humble veneration for the earth's providence is inseparable from their model of harmonious co-existence, rooted in gratitude itself.

Research shows the networks of kindness and appreciation scaling massively, not just due to people reciprocating good deeds, but by changing the societal atmosphere itself. The simple acts fuel each other, igniting expansive feedback loops of contagious generosity as the new norm.

At the most fundamental level, choosing to tune into deep gratitude for the gift of life catalyzes a shift in how we relate to everything. We start seeing the sacred worth in the tiniest joys - a hot shower after a long day, the priceless art of a honeybee pollinating, a baby's delighted eyes studying our face, the crisp sweetness of an apple providing nourishment. Our entire world becomes reanimated with sparkle and significance when we withhold nothing from our heartfelt sense of awe and thankfulness for all that nourishes us.

With this perspective, we experience the stunning generosity of this universe - that we get to sip our morning mug of warmth while watching sunlight blaze over the horizon. That we're gifted the ability to move our bodies through space like dancers redefining gravity with every step. That we possess these miraculous sensory portals to take in beauty through sight, scent, sound, taste. To witness the choreography of existence perpetually unfolding in spectacular fashion all around us.

Every single element of our astonishing existence - from the saltiness of our tears to the drumming of our hearts to the neural fireworks allowing us to perceive these words - was precisely hand-delivered to us as a gracious offering from life itself. To not express supreme gratitude for the totality of this experience is to numb ourselves to the utterly transcendent truth of just how fortunate we are.

So the next time you find yourself rushing from one obligation to the next without a moment's pause, stop. Close your eyes and simply feel your feet rooted into the nourishing support of the earth beneath you. Let your lungs drink the life-sustaining breath of this living planet. Feast your senses on each sight, sound, texture and fragrance. Leave absolutely no experience unacknowledged or untasted. Marinate in the raw gratitude of being as awake as your nervous system will allow.

Then watch as the universe bows with your humble reverence. As your spirit unleashes new reservoirs of brightness, your heart overflows with the beauty you once missed. As you slow down to honor this magnificent universe in awestruck thanksgiving, the universe rushes to dance with you in resonant appreciation.

For this is the highest state of living we can access - to exist as a radiant chrysalis of gratitude itself, feasted on the nourished received, endlessly celebrating the privilege of being. Always in love, always in awe, no experience too small to be swallowed whole with brimming gratefulness.

Go ahead, take a deep breath right now. Exhale out your rush and breathe in the simple splendor of being alive in this moment. Now go forth and let the entire universe be bathed in the unassailable light of your deepest gratitude.

**Here are 10 actionable insights on expressing deepest gratitude:**

1. Start a gratitude journal where you write down even the smallest things you're thankful for each day, like the beautiful sunset you saw on your drive home or your co-worker bringing you a coffee.

2. Set reminders to pause for a moment throughout the day and mindfully appreciate your surroundings through sight, sound, smell, etc., like noticing the birds chirping outside your window.

3. Before eating a meal, take a moment to express gratitude for the food and all the effort that went into growing, transporting, and preparing it.

4. Go for a hike, spend time tending to a garden, or find other ways to reconnect with nature and be awed by the natural world around you.

5. When someone shares what they're grateful for, listen attentively without jumping to respond, allowing them to fully express themselves.

6. Volunteer your time for a cause you care about, focusing on the gift of being able to help while also feeling inspired by the impact.

7. Notice habits or aspects of your life you may take for granted, like working eyes or a comfortable home, and consciously feel gratefulness for them.

8. Start each morning by expressing gratitude out loud for the new day and things you're thankful for in that moment, like waking up rested.

9. Learn from cultures that make gratitude rituals a sacred daily group practice, like holding a gratitude circle with loved ones.

10. Keep a "Gratitude Catalog" recording people you appreciate, acts of kindness you've received, and personal accomplishments to celebrate.

**20 questions to assess and remind yourself to practice gratitude:**

1. Do you make time to consciously reflect on what you're grateful for each day? For example, keep a gratitude journal and write down 3-5 things you're

thankful for before bed, like your pet's affection or a good workout.

2. How often do you express gratitude to others directly? Make it a habit to thank people face-to-face, like your bus driver or the cashier at the grocery store. A simple "Thank you for your help today" goes a long way.

3. Do you pause to feel gratitude for simple pleasures like a nice meal or beautiful day? When you eat your favorite food or see a vibrant sunset, take a moment to breathe deeply and savor the experience with appreciation.

4. When was the last time you took stock of basic aspects of life you may overlook, like running water or electricity? Think about how different your day would be without these amenities and be thankful for their reliable presence.

5. Do you find yourself complaining frequently? Notice when you start to complain about something and flip the script by verbally listing things you're grateful for in that situation instead.

6. Are you consciously thankful for challenges that help you grow? When you face a difficult situation like a job setback, view it as an opportunity and be grateful for the chance to develop resilience.

7. How attuned are you to your bodily sensations and thankful for your health? Pay attention to simple abilities like breathing easily or digesting food without discomfort, and appreciate your body's capabilities.

8. Do you make an effort to learn about others' perspectives and cultures? Educate yourself on traditions and worldviews different than your own to expand your horizons for experiencing gratefulness.

9. When you receive help or kindness, do you feel indebted or graciously accept the goodwill? Rather than feeling you owe something in return, simply receive the kind act with thankfulness.

10. Do you create gratitude rituals or reminders to stay grounded in appreciative awareness? Set a daily phone alert to pause and think about what you're thankful for in that moment.

11. Do you appreciate yourself and your accomplishments, not just others? Celebrate your own hard work by taking pride in goals you've achieved through diligence and being grateful for your efforts.

12. How often do you feel bitter, resentful or envious of others? When you notice these draining negative emotions, counter them by actively thinking of things you're thankful for.

13. Are you comfortable expressing vulnerability and thankfulness for emotional support? Voice appreciation to loved ones who provide a listening ear or words of encouragement during tough times.

14. Do you experience awe through connections with nature, art or spirituality? Spend time in parks, museums or places of worship to feel amazed by the world's beauty and be thankful for it.

15. In tough times, can you access gratitude as a coping strategy? When facing a challenge like illness or loss, focus on aspects of your life you're blessed to have, like supportive friends.

16. Do you pay gratitude forward by actively nurturing it in others? Model being thankful for family and friends by frequently expressing your appreciation for their presence in your life.

17. Are you able to feel appreciative joy when others experience good fortune? Rather than feeling jealous, genuinely delight in others' successes and be grateful for their happiness.

18. Do you take responsibility for your own gratitude practice? Realize that feeling grateful is an inside job that takes consistent work through habits like journaling or prayer/meditation.

19. Can you reframe failures as fortunate lessons? When you face a setback, view it as an opportunity that revealed areas to improve and be thankful for the wisdom gained.

20. Do your gratitude practices feel authentic and embodied, not forced? Make sure to practice from a place of sincerity so the feelings of thankfulness ring true within you.

The entire cosmos is perpetually offering itself to you in each moment for your reverent reception and thanksgiving. By choosing to show up in existential gratitude, you become a radiant claimant receiving and basking in that infinite bounty.

**Points from Neuroscience Quoted in Chapter 9: Deepest gratitude**

1. Impact of gratitude on neural activity:

Gratitude practices have been shown to produce tangible effects on brain activity.

2. MRI studies showing effects of gratitude practices:

MRI studies show gratitude practices produce powerful effects on the brain.

3. Increased dopamine production due to gratitude:

Gratitude practices lead to increased production of dopamine, a neurotransmitter associated with pleasure and reward.

4. Increased serotonin production from gratitude:

Practicing gratitude results in increased production of serotonin, a neurotransmitter linked to mood regulation and well-being.

5. Activation of the brain's bliss biosystem through gratitude:

Gratitude practices activate what the document refers to as "the brain's bliss biosystem".

6. Reduction of cortisol levels associated with gratitude:

Expressing gratitude is linked to reduced levels of cortisol, a hormone associated with stress.

7. Influence of grateful thoughts and sensations on neurochemistry:

Thoughts and sensations of gratefulness quite tangibly influence our neurochemistry in nourishing ways.

8. Counteraction of aging through gratitude's neural effects:

Gratitude practices can counteract aging at a neural level.

9. Reduction of anxiety at a neural level through gratitude:

Gratitude practices are said to reduce anxiety by altering neural activity.

10. Mitigation of disease through gratitude's impact on the brain:

Gratitude can help mitigate disease through its effects on the brain.

# Chapter 10
## Valuing our gifts

Can you feel an inner spark burning bright within you? That radiant essence aching to be fanned into full flame? Do you feel you have unique and divine gifts calling out to be expressed, to be celebrated, to be poured into this world.

Too often, we mute and ignore the sacred talents, skills, creativity and powers that make us uniquely, vibrantly us. We let societal pressures and narrow narratives dull the brilliance of our souls' deepest callings. We relegate our gifts to hobbies or side interests rather than anchoring into them as our truest offering to this life.

Does this resonate as a reminder for you - the world needs the full radiance of who you are. It needs the novel thoughts, insights and artistic expressions only you can create. It needs the problems only your mind can reframe and solve. It needs the synergy of your whole constellation of gifts woven together into the original masterpiece that is you, fully claimed.

I feel the evidence of this universal longing for us to step into our greatness everywhere around me. Take Rajnish, for instance. Growing up with undiagnosed ADHD, he felt constant shame about his struggles to focus in school. His extraordinary imagination and ability to hyperfocus on subjects that fired his curiosity were labeled as problems. It wasn't until a teacher pulled him aside to witness the breathtaking science-fiction stories Rajnish privately penned that he realized his "disabilities" were actually sacred callings to be heeded.

After embracing writing as a vital part of his purpose, Rajnish blossomed into a prolific author sparking conversations about humanity's unlimited potential. His books envision future worlds that inspire millions to cherish their own minds as keys to transcending our most daunting crises. By valuing his creative gifts, Rajnish catalyzed quantum leaps in human consciousness.

Then there's Rohan, a brilliant statistician born with high-functioning autism. For years he underutilized his capacity for mathematical patterning out of internalized impostor syndrome. It wasn't until a caring mentor reaffirmed the sacredness of Rohan's mind that he gave himself permission to flow in his abilities.

Today, his consultancy is helping companies and governments alike decode complex global supply chain issues through modern analytics. Meanwhile, his pioneering work decrypting the numerical language underlying our quantum universe is pushing the boundaries of science itself. Rohan's gifts turned him into a visionary, once he finally valued them as cosmic blessings.

We see this spiritual truth - that our distinctive talents and creative expressions are sacred callings - reflected across every human culture and wisdom tradition worldwide. From the revered Aboriginal concept of "dreamtime" or one's mythic leaning from the cosmos to Plato's theory of divine inspiration channeled through genius, indigenous worldviews have long understood giftedness as a divine blessing, not an accident.

The latest neuroscientific research backs this up, revealing that creative insights and lightning-in-a-bottle "aha moments" actually arise from regions of the brain linked to our highest potentials, our unconscious processing of symbolic knowledge, and states of epiphany-inducing bliss. When we give form to our gifts, we're literally accessing our cosmic brilliance.

At the collective level, imagine the quantum leap our civilization could experience if more of us chose to devote ourselves fully to this highest expression and valuing of our unique genius. If we unshackled ourselves from existences of mind-numbing routines and status quo to instead live by heeding to our souls' deepest callings. If we anchored into the belief that our gifts and powers - artistic or analytical, innovative or spiritual -

aren't just hobbies but threads of the very cosmic genius we're woven from.

We would be able to live at a deep and authentic level. Unharnessed creativity flourishing alongside technological breakthroughs. Inner awakenings multiplying across communities as more humans unbound themselves from conformity to instead live in service to their souls' highest artistic and innovative missives. We'd see unparalleled levels of individual thriving and human progression as each person embraced their deeper role in co-creating a more vibrant existence for us all.

Just look at the revolutionary makers and artists already modeling this liberated existence. Visionary painters, poets, musicians and weavers intentionally living as they seed our world with dazzling acts of imaginative resistance magically expressing their uniqueness. Their courageously expressed gifts are prototype blueprints for what an authentic human existence could look like as we all dismantle our internalized shackles and gift the world with our most elevated states of consciousness.

At our core, each of us is hardwired to value and give expression to our innate talents and creative callings. It's what allows us to reach our highest ecstatic states of flow and transcendent meaning. It's what helps us access deeper insights into our life's purpose while inspiring others to rise up into their greatest potentials too.

So if you've been listening to those whispers urging you toward vistas of untapped brilliance and artistry, I encourage you to heed them. Say yes to finally honoring those pieces of your sacred soul spark that have been yearning to catch fire and illuminate all of existence with their glow.

This can be your one exquisite life, or it can just be another existence of mistakenly playing small and safe. You were encoded with a unique bouquet of gifts and powers for a reason. What might be possible if we all had the courage to truly value them?

Let this be the invitation you've been waiting for. Step into the full unleashing of your soul's most vibrant potentials and highest artistry. The world is aching for your creative genius, yearning to experience existence through the unique cosmic lens only you can provide. So go ahead - unbridle those gifts in all your dazzling glory.

For when you value and pour the full vastness of who you are into this universe, you create pathways for us all to rise up together into the brilliance of our essential nature. What could be more sacred than that?

## 10 Actionable Insights on Valuing Your Gifts:

1. Know and celebrate your talents:

Keep a "success journal" where you write down your daily accomplishments, no matter how small. This practice helps you recognize and appreciate your skills regularly.

2. Adopt a growth mindset:

When faced with a challenge, instead of saying "I can't do this," try saying "I can't do this yet." This simple shift in language encourages learning and improvement.

3. Make efforts to realize your potential:

Set aside 30 minutes each day to work on a skill you want to improve. For example, if you want to become a better writer, practice writing a short story or article daily.

4. Tap into your subconscious mind:

Before sleep, ask your subconscious a question related to a problem you're trying to solve. Keep a notepad by your bed to jot down any insights upon waking.

5. Stretch your limits:

Take on a project slightly beyond your current skill level. If you're a beginner guitarist, try learning a moderately difficult song to push your abilities.

6. Recognize your gifts as blessings:

Start each day with a gratitude practice, acknowledging three ways your talents have positively impacted your life or others' lives.

7. Express your authentic self:

Incorporate your unique skills into your daily routine. If you're artistic, use your creativity to decorate your workspace or solve problems at work.

8. Develop your talents:

Allocate time each week for deliberate practice. If you're a public speaker, record yourself giving a speech and analyze areas for improvement.

9. Share your gifts with others:

Volunteer your skills to help someone in need. If you're good at math, offer to tutor a struggling student.

10. Embrace the joy of creation:

Engage in activities that allow you to use your talents purely for enjoyment. If you're musical, play your instrument just for fun without worrying about perfection.

Here are 20 questions to reflect on the progress made in valuing our gifts:

1. How often do I consciously acknowledge and appreciate my talents?

Explanation: This question encourages regular self-reflection and recognition of our abilities. Neuroscience research shows that practicing gratitude activates the brain's reward center, releasing dopamine and serotonin, which contribute to feelings of wellbeing. By consciously acknowledging our talents, we reinforce neural pathways associated with positive self-perception.

Example: Meera, a graphic designer, started keeping a "talent journal" where she wrote down one thing she did well each day. After a month, she noticed increased confidence in her abilities and was more likely to take on challenging projects at work.

2. In what ways have I challenged myself to grow my skills in the past month?

Explanation: This question promotes a growth mindset, which neuroscience research has shown to be crucial for learning and development. When we challenge ourselves, we create new neural connections and strengthen existing ones, a process known as neuroplasticity. This helps us adapt to new situations and improve our skills over time.

Example: Rahul, an amateur photographer, decided to learn a new photography technique each month. By consistently pushing himself out of his comfort zone, he not only improved his skills but also discovered new areas of interest within photography.

3. How have I used my talents to benefit others recently?

Explanation: Using our talents to help others activates the brain's reward system, releasing oxytocin, often called the "bonding hormone." This not only strengthens social connections but also reinforces the value of our gifts. Neuroimaging studies have shown that acts of altruism activate regions of the brain associated with pleasure and social connection.

Example: Malvika, a skilled baker, started volunteering at a local shelter once a month to teach baking classes. This not only allowed her to share her talent but also gave her a sense of purpose and community connection.

4. What new skill or talent have I discovered about myself lately?

Explanation: This question encourages ongoing self-discovery and openness to new experiences. Neuroscience research shows that learning new skills creates new neural pathways and can even increase the density of white matter in the brain, which is associated with improved cognitive function.

Example: Tarun, who always considered himself "non-musical," decided to try a ukulele class on a whim. To his surprise, he found he had a natural sense of rhythm and enjoyed creating music, opening up a whole new area of personal growth.

5. How have I incorporated my talents into my daily routine?

Explanation: Regularly using our talents reinforces neural pathways associated with those skills, making them stronger and more efficient over time. This process, known as myelination, helps us perform tasks more easily and effectively. By incorporating our talents into daily life, we continually strengthen these neural connections.

Example: Lavanya, a natural organizer, applied her skills to create efficient systems for her home and work life. She found that this not only made her more productive but also reduced her stress levels and increased her overall satisfaction.

6. In what ways have I stretched my comfort zone using my talents?

Explanation: Pushing our boundaries activates the brain's stress response system, releasing cortisol and adrenaline. While too much stress can be harmful, moderate levels of these hormones can enhance focus and performance. By stretching our comfort zone, we train our brains to handle challenges more effectively over time.

Example: Arun, an introvert who excels at writing, pushed himself to give a presentation at a local writers' group. Although nervous at first, he found that sharing his knowledge boosted his confidence and opened up new opportunities for collaboration.

7. How have I celebrated my achievements, both big and small?

Explanation: Celebrating achievements, no matter how small, triggers the release of dopamine in the brain's reward center. This reinforces the behavior that led to the achievement and motivates us to continue developing our talents. Neuroscience research shows that this positive reinforcement is crucial for habit formation and long-term skill development.

Example: Vineeta started a "victory jar" where she wrote down her achievements on small pieces of paper. At the end of each month, she read through them, allowing herself to fully appreciate her progress and motivating her to set new goals.

8. What steps have I taken to learn more about my areas of talent?

Explanation: Actively seeking knowledge about our talents engages the brain's curiosity centers, releasing dopamine and promoting continued learning. This process of active learning strengthens neural connections related to our talents and can lead to the formation of new connections, expanding our capabilities.

Example: Madhu, a hobby gardener, started attending local horticultural society meetings and reading botany books. This deepened his understanding of plant biology, allowing him to apply scientific principles to his gardening and significantly improve his results.

9. How have I used my talents to solve a problem or overcome a challenge recently?

Explanation: Problem-solving using our talents engages the brain's executive function centers, particularly the prefrontal cortex. This strengthens our ability to apply our skills in novel situations and promotes cognitive flexibility. Neuroscience research shows that this type of creative problem-solving can even generate new neurons in the hippocampus, a process known as neurogenesis.

Example: Abhimanyu, a skilled negotiator, used his talents to mediate a dispute between two colleagues at work. By applying his skills in a new context, he not only resolved the conflict but also gained new insights into group dynamics.

10. In what ways have I combined different talents or skills to create something new?

Explanation: Combining different skills activates multiple areas of the brain simultaneously, creating new neural connections between these regions. This process, known as cognitive synthesis, can lead to innovative ideas and solutions. Neuroscience research suggests that this type of creative thinking can improve overall cognitive function and mental flexibility.

Example: Raghu, who had skills in both programming and music, created a new app that helps musicians compose by suggesting chord progressions based on music theory algorithms. This project allowed him to merge his passions in a unique and fulfilling way.

11. How have I sought feedback on my talents and used it for improvement?

Explanation: Seeking and processing feedback activates regions of the brain associated with self-awareness and social cognition. This helps us develop a more accurate self-perception and identify areas for growth. Neuroscience research shows that constructive feedback can stimulate neuroplasticity, allowing us to adapt and improve our skills more effectively.

Example: Jahnavi, an aspiring chef, started a cooking blog where she encouraged readers to provide honest feedback on her recipes. By actively seeking and incorporating this feedback, she was able to refine her cooking techniques and develop more appealing recipes.

12. What opportunities have I created or seized to showcase my talents?

Explanation: Creating opportunities to showcase our talents engages the brain's reward system, releasing dopamine and reinforcing confidence in our abilities. This positive reinforcement can motivate us to continue developing and sharing our skills. Neuroimaging studies have shown that anticipation of positive outcomes activates the same reward centers as actually experiencing those outcomes.

Example: Rohit, a talented amateur bird photographer, organized a local exhibition of his work at a prominent gallery in Mumbai. This not only allowed him to share his art with others but also led to interesting conversations, connections and several projects, further validating his skills.

13. How have I adapted my talents to new or changing circumstances?

Explanation: Adapting our talents to new situations engages the brain's cognitive flexibility, a key component of executive function. This process strengthens neural pathways associated with problem-solving and creativity.

Neuroscience research suggests that this type of adaptive thinking can increase the density of gray matter in regions associated with decision-making and emotional regulation.

Example: Mallika, a yoga instructor, quickly adapted her in-person classes to an online format during the pandemic. This not only allowed her to continue teaching but also expanded her reach to students in different geographical locations.

14. In what ways have I used my talents to express my authentic self?

Explanation: Expressing our authentic selves through our talents activates the brain's reward centers and reduces activity in areas associated with anxiety and stress. This alignment between our inner selves and outer expression can lead to increased feelings of wellbeing and life satisfaction. Neuroscience research has shown that authenticity is associated with increased activation in the prefrontal cortex, an area involved in self-awareness and decision-making.

Example: Carlos, who had always suppressed his artistic side due to family pressure to pursue a "practical" career, started dedicating weekends to painting. This authentic expression of his talent not only improved his mood but also led to a sense of fulfillment he hadn't experienced before.

15. How have I mentored or inspired others to develop their own talents?

Explanation: Mentoring others engages the brain's empathy and social cognition networks, releasing oxytocin and promoting feelings of connection. This not only reinforces our own skills but also provides a new perspective on our talents. Neuroscience research suggests that teaching others can enhance our own learning and memory consolidation through a process called the "protégé effect."

Example: Radha, an experienced software developer, started a coding club for high school students. By explaining concepts to others, she deepened her own understanding and gained fresh insights into her field.

16. What steps have I taken to overcome self-doubt or imposter syndrome regarding my talents?

Explanation: Overcoming self-doubt involves retraining our brain's habitual thought patterns, a process that engages neuroplasticity. By consciously challenging negative self-talk, we can weaken neural pathways associated with self-doubt and strengthen those associated with confidence. Neuroscience research has shown that practices like positive self-affirmation can reduce activity in the brain's threat-response centers.

Example: Despite being a skilled writer, Arjun often doubted his abilities. He started keeping a "proof of competence" folder where he saved positive feedback and evidence of his successes. Reviewing this folder regularly helped him combat imposter syndrome and build confidence in his talents.

17. How have I integrated mindfulness or meditation practices to enhance my talents?

Explanation: Mindfulness and meditation practices have been shown to increase gray matter density in brain regions associated with learning, memory, and emotional regulation. These practices can also reduce activity in the default mode network, which is associated with mind-wandering and self-referential thoughts. By incorporating mindfulness, we can improve focus and reduce performance anxiety related to our talents.

Example: Lakshmi, a trained classical musician, incorporated a 10-minute mindfulness practice before each performance. This helped her manage pre-performance anxiety and improved her ability to stay present and focused during recitals.

18. In what ways have I collaborated with others to amplify or complement my talents?

Explanation: Collaboration engages the brain's social cognition networks and can lead to the release of oxytocin, promoting bonding and trust. Working with others also exposes us to diverse perspectives, stimulating cognitive flexibility and creativity. Neuroscience research suggests that collaborative problem-solving can lead to more innovative solutions than individual work.

Example: Sachin, a graphic designer, partnered with a copywriter friend to offer comprehensive branding services. This collaboration not only expanded their business opportunities but also pushed both to grow in their respective fields.

19. How have I used visualization or mental rehearsal to enhance my talents?

Explanation: Visualization activates many of the same neural pathways as actually performing a task. This mental rehearsal can strengthen neural connections associated with our talents, improving performance and confidence. Neuroscience research has shown that visualization can enhance motor skills, reduce anxiety, and improve focus.

Example: Maya, a competitive swimmer, incorporated daily visualization exercises into her training routine. She would mentally rehearse her races, imagining every detail from the start to the finish. This practice helped her improve her times and manage pre-race nerves more effectively.

20. What long-term goals have I set to further develop and apply my talents?

Explanation: Setting long-term goals activates the brain's motivation and planning centers, particularly the prefrontal cortex. This process of envisioning the future and planning steps to achieve it can increase dopamine levels, motivating us to take action. Neuroscience research suggests that having clear, meaningful goals can enhance overall cognitive function and life satisfaction.

Example: Robin, an amateur musician, set a five-year goal to compose and perform an original piece at a local music festival. This long-term vision motivated him to consistently practice and study music theory, leading to steady improvement in his skills and creativity.

By regularly reflecting on these questions and actively working to value and develop our gifts, we can create lasting positive changes in our brains and lives. The brain's plasticity means that we have the ability to grow and adapt throughout our lives. Embracing and developing our talents is not just a matter of skill acquisition, but a journey of self-discovery and personal growth.

Your gifts and powers are notes of a celestial song that's been playing since the dawn of this universe's creation. Yours is the voice that can finally help it reach its crescendo and reverberate its sublime majesty back through all of existence. By celebrating our talents, we are answering the call to follow our deepest calling.

# List of neuroscience concepts and research quoted in Chapter 10: Valuing our gifts

1. Gratitude practice activates the brain's reward center, releasing dopamine and serotonin.

2. Growth mindset is crucial for learning and development, promoting neuroplasticity.

3. Challenging ourselves creates new neural connections and strengthens existing ones.

4. Acts of altruism activate brain regions associated with pleasure and social connection.

5. Learning new skills creates new neural pathways and can increase white matter density in the brain.

6. Regular use of talents reinforces and strengthens associated neural pathways through myelination.

7. Moderate stress levels can enhance focus and performance by releasing cortisol and adrenaline.

8. Celebrating achievements triggers dopamine release in the brain's reward center.

9. Active learning strengthens neural connections and can lead to the formation of new connections.

10. Problem-solving engages the brain's executive function centers, particularly the prefrontal cortex.

11. Creative problem-solving can generate new neurons in the hippocampus (neurogenesis).

12. Combining different skills activates multiple brain areas simultaneously, creating new neural connections (cognitive synthesis).

13. Seeking and processing feedback activates regions associated with self-awareness and social cognition.

14. Anticipation of positive outcomes activates the same reward centers as experiencing those outcomes.

15. Adaptive thinking can increase gray matter density in regions associated with decision-making and emotional regulation.

16. Authentic self-expression activates brain reward centers and reduces activity in areas associated with anxiety and stress.

17. Teaching others enhances our own learning and memory consolidation (the "protégé effect").

18. Positive self-affirmation can reduce activity in the brain's threat-response centers.

19. Mindfulness and meditation practices can increase gray matter density in brain regions associated with learning, memory, and emotional regulation.

20. Meditation can reduce activity in the default mode network, associated with mind-wandering and self-referential thoughts.

21. Collaboration engages the brain's social cognition networks and can lead to oxytocin release.

22. Visualization activates many of the same neural pathways as actually performing a task.

23. Setting long-term goals activates the brain's motivation and planning centers, particularly the prefrontal cortex.

24. The brain's plasticity allows for growth and adaptation throughout life.

.

## Chapter 11
## Change, attachment, letting go

Can you feel the currents of life swirling all around you? That relentless ebb and flow of beginnings and endings, arrivals and departures, gains and losses? Change is the only constant in this human experience we share.

Yet for so many of us, that inevitable flux fills us with anxiety, fear and desperation to control what is ultimately uncontrollable. We become overly attached to specific plans, relationships, identities - believing that's where our safety and happiness lie. And when those inevitably start shifting, as all things must, we fight like hell to freeze that fleeting moment in time.

But what if instead of calcifying around the impermanent, we found ways to swim fluidly with the stream? To gracefully let go of what's already cresting behind us so we can surrender ourselves to the new waves perpetually coming our way?

I've witnessed firsthand how this art of "detached allowing" is one of the bravest, most liberated ways to move through this life. Like with Amara, a woman who thought she had it all - successful career, beautiful family, picture-perfect lifestyle. Until her shocking divorce and job loss sent everything crumbling, leaving her questioning her entire identity.

Crushed by the loss of her attachments, Amara fell into deep depression until she started seeing a counselor trained in Buddhist principles around impermanence and non-attachment to help her reframe the suffering. As she slowly released the white-knuckled grip she had on all those external circumstances she'd mistakenly anchored herself to, she opened to profound new insights around her innate resilience and wholeness beyond any role or title. Yes, mourning losses is natural. But she learned to stop compounding the pain by mentally clinging to the mirage of permanence. Each time she put down that heavy baggage of attachment, she felt lighter, free to flow fearlessly with life's changing tides.

That lesson hit home for me too when I suddenly lost a beloved family member with little warning. The earth dissolved beneath my feet as reality shattered. And for awhile, I desperately grasped at anything to regain a sense of stability - replaying memories, obsessively avoiding reminders of their absence, angrily interrogating why they had to leave so soon.

It was torturous. Until finally, through my haze of anguish, I remembered - our existences are written in sand, washed away and reshaped by each incoming wave.

To cling to a static imprint in that sand is to dull my senses to the profound gift of the ever-shifting, ever-recreating present moment. Once I made space to fully grieve yet release my attachment to a person frozen in time, new openings for awe, sweetness and celebration blossomed within me again. Their energy shape-shifted into boundless love, alive within me, agile and whole.

Science validates how vital this ability to let go is for our mental health and inner freedom. Research shows the neurological hallmarks of attachment fuel the fear circuitry in our brain's amygdala. The more we desperately grip at a static identity, circumstance or possession, the more we atrophy the neural pathways wired for growth, acceptance and resilience. Moreover, our heart rhythm patterns become more erratic and cortisol levels spike when we can't let go of attachments, impacting immunity, longevity and overall wellbeing.

But by learning to practice non-attachment through exercises like meditation, breathwork and self-inquiry, we steadily dissolve the calcified ego's anxious stranglehold so we can flow with the currents of impermanence, even amidst life's most disruptive plot twists. We strengthen the muscle of equanimity so that no matter what waves come crashing in, we can ride them with grace rather than rigid panic.

It's a constant dance of coming to center in the one constant we can rely on – this living, breathing present moment – while simultaneously blessing and releasing what has already drifted behind us. From this anchored, non-attached presence, we can remain malleable, resilient and ever-opening to life's unfolding mystery rather than suffering over its inevitable shape-shifts.

We see powerful examples of people embodying this liberating principle through extremely difficult circumstances. Like Jake, a recent widower who's learned to honor his wife's spirit through celebrating her life rather than bitterly clinging to physical attachment and sorrow around her death. Or Mai-Ling, whose refugee past taught her to embrace change and letting go as portals for spiritual growth, helping her agilely ground in new chapters with trust rather than catastrophic fear.

Then there are the cultural torchbearers preserving time-honored wisdom traditions around fluidity and flow. The Indigenous Bri Bri of Costa Rica, for instance, start teaching non-attachment to their children from a young age through gentle practices like building sandcastles on the beach and watching each one dissolve back into the ocean. When the waves inevitably return to sweep the sand anew, the elders use that as a visceral lesson in the impermanence of all material forms while instilling reverence for the constant cycle of death and rebirth.

Meanwhile, the Buddhist monastics in places like Bhutan devote themselves to sacred contemplation of anitya – the liberating understanding that every emotion, experience, possession and relationship is by nature momentary and impermanent. They anchor into this truth through rituals letting go of fixation on attachment and aversion, dissolving the perceptual boundaries around what they believe is permanent and not. As they do, they access vast oceans of inner peace and spiritual freedom, able to embrace all of life and death without clinging to anything arising.

At its essence, practicing this mindset of allowing change while releasing our toxic attachments is about dissolving the artificial fears, anxieties and delusions that cause so much of our unnecessary suffering. It's about fully surrendering ourselves to the cyclical flow of this universe's natural rhythms so we can live in bold trust and playfulness with reality.

It's about no longer letting the stories we cling to around who we are or how our lives are "supposed" to go limit our access to the full spectrum of joy, abundance and possibility always blossoming before us. With open, unattached hands, we can fully grasp and relish this one great gift of existence we've been given.

So if you're moving through a season of disruptive change right now or still carrying the baggage of stale attachments and old identities you cling to out of habit, let this be your invitation to set down those heavy burdens. Let this act of surrender be the sacred gesture that lets life breathe a new story through you, fresh with excitement and limitless potential.

Change is not a calamity to be feared and resisted. It liberates us from all those pockets of stagnation we have been sleepwalking through. It is a great reminder that nothing, and no one, truly belongs to you with permanent possession. By embracing impermanence, you open yourself to partake in a continual stream of reciprocal becoming, shedding old skins for births infinitely resurrecting again.

Learning to meet it all - the comings and goings, the velvet cradlings and all the leavings - with the same open, detached embrace. By refusing to stash anything away in psychic lock-boxes of attachment or shut down any possibility for growth through denial, you'll discover the ultimate inner freedom that waits on the riverbank of pure presence, just this side of the next horizon's turn.

And trust me, when you start flowing from that agile, spacious vibration of letting go, everything about your entire life becomes profoundly transformed. How liberating it is to grasp fully at nothing, hold tightly to no fixed story—so that each new encounter and chapter is free to spark fresh wonder, totally unburdened. You become endlessly shaped and reshaped by that grand cosmic potter, more alive than you've ever known.

So go ahead, release your grip on the familiar, beloved and known. Loosen your attachments and meet the mystery of this emerging moment with a welcoming exhale. For this—the delicious giving and receiving, the constant recreation of reality into previously unimagined forms—is your soul's eternal birthright to dance with.

**Here are 10 actionable insights, with case studies and explanations on change and letting go:**

1. Start a daily meditation or breathwork practice to anchor you in the still point of presence beyond attachment.

Example: Anuradha, a busy executive, started a 10-minute daily meditation practice. She focused on her breath, observing thoughts without judgment. Over time, she noticed she was less reactive to work stress and more able to detach from anxious thoughts about the future. The practice helped her stay grounded in the present moment, reducing her tendency to cling to outcomes or worry excessively about change.

2. Notice when you're mentally rehearsing storylines of cravings or aversions around desired/dreaded outcomes. Let them pass.

Example: Shekhar was anxiously awaiting news about a job promotion. He caught himself constantly imagining both positive and negative scenarios. Recognizing this pattern, he started to acknowledge these thoughts without engaging them. "There's that story about getting rejected again," he'd note, then gently redirect his attention to the present task. This practice helped reduce his anxiety and attachment to a specific outcome.

3. Before making commitments or intensifying bonds, consciously check in for any neurotic clinginess fueling the motivation.

Example: Amita was considering getting into a new relationship. Before making the decision, she took time to reflect on her motivations. She realized part of her eagerness stemmed from a fear of being alone rather than a genuine desire for shared living. Recognizing this, she decided to work on her independence before taking this step, leading to a healthier relationship dynamic.

4. Engage in practices like spending time in nature to build reverence for the natural cycles of birth, death and regeneration.

Example: Karan, struggling with the loss of a loved one, started taking weekly hikes in a nearby forest. Observing the changing seasons, fallen leaves nurturing new growth, and the constant flux of nature helped him gain perspective on life's cycles. This practice fostered acceptance of change and impermanence, easing his grief process.

5. Do a daily "letting go" ritual of naming what you release attachment to - write it down, speak it aloud, burn it, etc.

Example: Reema adopted a nightly ritual of writing down one thing she needed to release on a small piece of paper. Whether it was a grudge, a fear, or an expectation, she would then burn the paper in a small, safe container. This symbolic act helped her consciously practice letting go, gradually reducing her tendency to hold onto negative emotions and rigid expectations.

6. Anytime you're in a transitional period, create ceremonies to consciously mark the ending of one chapter before the next begins.

Example: When Alex was leaving his job of 10 years for a new opportunity, he organized a small ceremony with close colleagues. They shared memories, expressed gratitude, and Alex symbolically "handed over" his responsibilities. This ritual provided closure, allowing Alex to fully embrace his new role without lingering attachments to his old position.

7. Keep a gratitude journal focusing not on possessing things, but experiencing humble appreciation for this transitional human life.

Example: Sandhya started a daily gratitude practice, focusing on experiences rather than possessions. She'd write about the warmth of sunlight, a kind stranger's smile, or the taste of her morning coffee. Over time, this shifted her focus from acquiring things to appreciating fleeting moments, fostering a sense of contentment and reducing her attachment to material possessions.

8. Study spiritual texts that emphasize non-attachment and flowing like water as pathways to inner freedom.

Example: Thomas, feeling stuck in his life, began studying Buddhism and Eastern philosophies. The concept of "wu wei" or effortless action resonated with him. He started practicing going with the flow of life rather than constantly striving and grasping. This study and practice helped him release his rigid expectations and find more peace in uncertainty.

9. Notice when you're seeking permanence through consumption - let each experience be impermanent and sufficient in itself.

Example: Aradhya realized she had a habit of online shopping when stressed, seeking the momentary high of a new purchase. She began to pause before buying, asking herself if she was trying to fill an emotional void. Instead, she would fully engage in a present moment activity, like savoring a cup of tea. This practice helped her break the cycle of seeking fulfillment through consumption.

10. Intentionally befriend your fears of uncertainty and the unknown by journaling about their roots and releasing each layer.

Example: Manpreet, facing a major career change, started journaling about his fears of the unknown. He traced these fears back to childhood experiences of instability. By acknowledging and exploring these roots, he was able to see his current situation more objectively. This process helped him release layers of anxiety and approach the change with more openness and curiosity.

**Here are questions for 20 self-assessment that would help to review current progress as well as provide pointers on coping with change and letting go:**

1. How often do I find myself dwelling on past events or worrying about the future instead of being present in the moment?

Example: Devi noticed she spent a lot of time replaying arguments with her partner or imagining worst-case scenarios at work. She started using a mindfulness app to track her present-moment awareness. Over time, she saw a decrease in rumination and an increase in her ability to focus on the here and now.

2. Can I identify three specific instances in the past week where I practiced letting go of something I couldn't control?

Example: Jay reflected on his week and realized he had let go of his frustration over a delayed flight, accepted a colleague's different working style without trying to change it, and released his expectation of perfect weather for a planned outdoor event. This awareness helped him recognize his growing capacity for acceptance.

3. How do I typically react to unexpected changes in my plans or routines?

Example: Latha noticed that she often became irritable and anxious when her daily routine was disrupted. She started experimenting with intentionally changing small parts of her routine, like taking a different route to work or trying a new breakfast food. This practice helped her build flexibility and reduce stress when facing unexpected changes.

4. In what areas of my life do I tend to hold onto things (physical, emotional, or mental) long after they've served their purpose?

Example: Kapil realized he had a habit of keeping old clothes he never wore, holding grudges against former friends, and clinging to outdated beliefs about his capabilities. He started a decluttering process - physically with his closet, emotionally by practicing forgiveness, and mentally by challenging his limiting beliefs.

5. How often do I pause to appreciate the present moment without trying to capture or prolong it?

Example: Isha noticed she constantly took photos of beautiful moments to post on social media. She challenged herself to experience one beautiful thing each day without documenting it. This practice helped her develop a deeper appreciation for the impermanence of moments and reduced her need to "possess" experiences.

6. Can I list five things I'm genuinely grateful for today that are not material possessions?

Example: Anirudh struggled with this at first, realizing how much he tied his happiness to things he owned. He started a gratitude practice, focusing on experiences and relationships. Over time, he found it easier to appreciate intangibles like a peaceful morning, a heartfelt conversation with a friend, or the satisfaction of solving a problem at work.

7. How do I cope with the feeling of uncertainty in various aspects of my life?

Example: Mala recognized that she often tried to control every aspect of her life to avoid uncertainty. She began practicing "planned uncertainty" by occasionally letting someone else choose the restaurant for dinner or taking a day trip without a set itinerary. These experiences helped her build tolerance for the unknown and reduce anxiety about unpredictability.

8. In what ways do I try to find security or permanence in impermanent things or situations?

Example: Prashant realized he often sought security through his job title and salary. When faced with a potential layoff, he recognized the impermanence of these external factors. He started developing internal sources of security, like building diverse skills and nurturing supportive relationships, which helped him feel more stable regardless of job circumstances.

9. How often do I compare my journey to others' and feel dissatisfied with my own progress?

Example: Aruna noticed that she frequently compared her career progress to her college classmates on LinkedIn, often feeling inadequate. She decided to limit her social media use and focus on setting personal growth goals based on her own values and aspirations. This shift helped her feel more content with her unique path and less attached to external markers of success.

10. Can I recall a recent situation where I responded to a challenge with flexibility and openness rather than resistance?

Example: Rahul remembered a project at work that took an unexpected direction. Instead of pushing for his original plan, he listened to his team's ideas and incorporated them, leading to a more innovative solution. Recognizing this instance of flexibility boosted his confidence in handling future uncertainties.

11. How do I handle goodbyes or endings in various areas of my life?

Example: Deepika realized she often avoided proper goodbyes, whether leaving a job or ending a relationship, because they felt too painful. She started creating small rituals for endings, like writing a gratitude letter or having a closure conversation. These practices helped her acknowledge the importance of transitions and move forward more easily.

12. In what ways do I try to control outcomes instead of focusing on my own actions and responses?

Example: Jayant noticed he spent a lot of energy trying to influence his children's choices rather than supporting their autonomy. He began focusing more on modeling the values he wanted to instill and being a supportive presence, rather than dictating their decisions. This shift improved his relationships and reduced his stress about outcomes.

13. How often do I take time to reflect on and release emotional baggage from past experiences?

Example: Veena realized she was carrying resentment from a past relationship into her current one. She started a journaling practice to explore these feelings and gradually release them. Over time, she found herself more present and trusting in her current relationship, unburdened by past hurts.

14. Can I identify three personal beliefs or habits that no longer serve me but I'm hesitant to let go of?

Example: Manish recognized that his belief in always being busy as a sign of productivity, his habit of saying yes to every request, and his reluctance to delegate were no longer serving him. He started challenging these patterns by scheduling downtime, practicing saying no, and trusting his team with important tasks. These changes led to better work-life balance and more effective leadership.

15. How do I respond to feedback or criticism? Can I separate my sense of self-worth from external opinions?

Example: Shweta noticed she often felt devastated by critical feedback at work. She began practicing receiving feedback with curiosity rather than defensiveness, and reminding herself that her worth wasn't determined by others' opinions. This approach helped her grow professionally while maintaining emotional stability.

16. In what ways do I attach my happiness to future events or achievements rather than finding contentment in the present?

Example: Ram realized he often thought, "I'll be happy when I get that promotion" or "Life will be perfect once I buy a house." He started a daily practice of noting three things he appreciated about his current situation. This helped him find more joy in the present while still working towards future goals.

17. How often do I practice self-compassion when facing setbacks or perceived failures?

Example: Maya noticed she was very hard on herself when things didn't go as planned. She began practicing self-compassion by treating herself with the same kindness she'd offer a friend facing a similar situation. This approach helped her bounce back from setbacks more quickly and reduced her fear of failure.

18. Can I recall a time when a perceived negative change or loss ultimately led to positive growth or new opportunities?

Example: Tarun reflected on losing a job he thought was perfect for him. Initially devastated, he now recognized how this led him to start his own business, which aligned better with his values and allowed more personal freedom. This reflection helped him approach future changes with more optimism and openness.

19. How do I balance setting goals and having aspirations with being content with what is?

Example: Vijaya struggled with always focusing on the next goal without appreciating her current achievements. She started a practice of celebrating small wins and finding satisfaction in the process of working towards goals, not just their completion. This helped her maintain motivation while also enjoying the present.

20. In what ways do I embrace the concept of impermanence in my daily life?

Example: Daya began consciously noting the changing seasons, the growth of his children, and the evolving nature of his work projects. He started taking photos of beautiful but temporary things like a sunset or a sandcastle. This practice helped him appreciate the beauty of impermanence and reduce his tendency to cling to static states in his life.

These questions and examples provide a comprehensive framework for self-assessment and growth in the areas of change, attachment, and letting go. By regularly reflecting on these questions and implementing the insights gained, individuals can develop greater flexibility, resilience, and peace in the face of life's constant changes.

**List of Neuroscience concepts and research cited in chapter 11: Change, attachment, letting go**

1. Neural pathways related to growth, acceptance, and resilience: Brain circuits that can be strengthened through practices like meditation, breathwork, and self-inquiry.

2. Fear circuitry in the brain's amygdala: A region of the brain activated by attachment, potentially increasing fear responses.

3. Atrophy of neural pathways due to attachment: Excessive attachment to static identities or circumstances may weaken brain circuits associated with growth and adaptability.

4. Erratic heart rhythm patterns: Difficulty in letting go of attachments can lead to irregular cardiovascular functioning.

5. Cortisol level spikes linked to attachment: Inability to release attachments may trigger increased production of the stress hormone cortisol.

6. Impact of attachment on immunity, longevity, and overall wellbeing: Persistent attachment behaviors can negatively affect various aspects of physical health and lifespan.

## Chapter 12
## Purpose and a reason for a meaningful life

Can you feel that gentle tug, that subtle whisper reverberating through your soul? It's the call of your life's deepest purpose trying to get your attention. A sacred summons from something greater than the temporary and the immediate. An invitation to step into the mystery and embrace the reason you were given this one precious life.

Too many of us slog through our days disconnected from that profound sense of meaning. We get so bogged down in routines, expectations and distractions that we miss the miraculous essence animating us all along. Purpose - that orienting north star that fills our spirit and propels us into our most alive, authentic expression - gets lost amidst the noise and busyness.

But what if we slowed down and allowed ourselves to truly tune into that timeless resonance? To listen for those openings into our soul's secret passageways and untapped potentials? For those who've tasted the clarity of an existence married to purpose, it is utterly life-changing.

I've seen it radiate through friends like Aman, who endured a decade feeling aimless and depressed until he finally started heeding the creative sparks urging him to pick up a paintbrush again. As he lovingly nurtured his long-stifled calling to create visionary artworks expressing his cultural lineage, everything shifted. Aman emerged into his highest self-expression and service, merging activism with ethereal beauty in ways that now inspire thousands.

Or take Koshi, my dear friend who stumbled through years of self-destructive behaviors until he finally surrendered to his spirit's nudges to support others in overcoming addiction and trauma. Once he embraced that sacred purpose, Koshi's entire trajectory realigned to his destiny of becoming a healer helping transform intergenerational suffering.

Beneath our fleeting roles, ambitions or societal labels, each of us contains an inner essence encoded with specific gifts, perspectives and cosmic instructions for manifesting higher expressions of truth, beauty, healing and love in this world. When we live divorced from that inner compass, it keeps us trapped in existences of quiet desperation, burnout and feeling empty inside.

But the moment we start awakening to those shimmering threads of our soul's true callings? Everything we experience gets infused with vibrant new meaning and magic. Life feels effortlessly guided by energies far more vast than our small, personal myths. We step into current with the tides of destiny itself.

The latest neuroscience research illuminates what wisdom traditions have long known - that realizing our deepest purpose activates profoundly blissful brain states while heightening our sense of wholeness and connection to all life. Studies show that discovering personal meaning correlates with enhancements in psychological wellbeing, physical health, longevity, self-transcendental values, flow states, and more. It literally optimizes our entire system's functioning.

At the collective level, imagine the miraculous advancements we could birth if more people lived grounded in that divine directive whispering through them? Rather than masses coasting through lives of distraction or resignation, we'd see creative visionaries stepping up as architects of regenerative systems. We'd have communities prioritizing mentorship to ensure every child's unique brilliance was given space to blossom. Entire workforces of people showing up fully inspired, rather than disengaged, because their work was tied to the truest expression of their purpose.

We already see glimpses of the profound shifts possible through people actualizing their soul's reason for being here. Like Deepika, who against all odds and lack of resources, found her purpose in solving the clean water crisis decimating her rural village in North India. She innovated a low-cost portable nanotechnology to purify polluted groundwater supplies, uplifting countless communities while inspiring young girls everywhere to step into their STEM leadership.

At our core, this innate longing for purpose is hardwired into our psyche. Like a tree hardcoded with the cosmic intelligence to reach for the sun's light while sending roots into the earth for sustenance. Like the salmon instinctively knowing where to migrate each year to carry out their life's reason for being. Our entire existence as a species has been shaped by our ancient ancestors' unyielding devotion to purpose – whether creating civilizations, pioneering lifesaving inventions, safeguarding future generations or birthing philosophies that expanded human consciousness.

So if you've been feeling unmoored or restless, as if some part of you has been sleepwalking through the motions, recognize those stirrings as sacred signals from your soul, yearning to reawaken to life's deepest meaning and reason. Open yourself to receiving the subtle callings and synchronicities illuminating your unique path of joyful service, profound contribution and divine purpose.

For when you finally let yourself be consumed by that sense of ultimate meaning, everything internal and external starts shapeshifting in miraculous ways. Challenges no longer feel like burdensome hurdles, but initiations into higher awareness and purpose activation. Each breath and interaction becomes charged with intentionality and reverberance for a life contributing to a meaningful future. You dissolve back into the intricate choreography of nature's genius unfolding in perfect order.

So if you feel that sacred pulse within you to the beat of destiny's drum, turn towards it. Slow down, soften your receptive channels and give yourself over to the universal intelligence trying to stream its purpose through your distinctive form in this great creation story we're all co-authoring together.

This is the path to lives overflowing with meaning, resonance and soul-awakening – steadily attuning ourselves to our inner compass and then bravely following where it leads, even when the way seems uncertain. Because deep inside you know where you are meant to go. Your only job is to listen, trust and say yes to living in alignment with its promptings, no matter how unconventional or wildly they manifest.

This world aches for the brilliance of your most purposeful expression. What greater gift is there than heeding that sacred call and letting your life be a consecration of that highest reason reverberating within you? The universe awaits your "yes."

**Here are 10 actionable exercises that can help clarify one's purpose and find deeper meaning in life, along with practical examples and elaborations:**

1. Identify Your Values: Make a list of your core values—the principles and beliefs that are most important to you. Reflect on how you can better align your daily actions with these values. For example, if family is a core value, you might prioritize quality time with loved ones or make efforts to strengthen those bonds.

2. Explore Your Passions: Think about the activities, hobbies, or causes that truly excite and energize you. Consider how you can incorporate more of these into your life or even turn them into a vocation. For instance, if you're passionate about environmental conservation, you could volunteer with local organizations or pursue a career in that field.

3. Practice Gratitude: Make a daily habit of reflecting on things you're grateful for, no matter how small. Gratitude cultivates a positive mindset and helps you appreciate the present moment. You could start a gratitude journal, share gratitude with loved ones, or simply take a few minutes each day to silently acknowledge what you're thankful for.

4. Engage in Service: Find ways to contribute to something larger than yourself by volunteering, supporting a cause you care about, or helping others in need. This could involve mentoring youth, participating in community service projects, or donating your time or resources to a charitable organization.

5. Seek Personal Growth: Identify areas where you'd like to grow and develop, whether it's learning a new skill, pursuing a hobby, or exploring different philosophies or belief systems. Continuously challenging yourself and expanding your knowledge can deepen your sense of purpose and self-awareness.

6. Cultivate Meaningful Relationships: Invest time and energy into nurturing your most important relationships—with family, friends, or a romantic partner. Prioritize quality time, open communication, and shared experiences that strengthen these connections and bring more meaning to your life.

7. Connect with Nature: Spend time in natural environments, whether it's going for a hike, visiting a park, or simply sitting outdoors. Connecting with nature can foster a sense of awe, wonder, and appreciation for the world around you, which can contribute to a deeper sense of purpose.

8. Practice Mindfulness: Incorporate mindfulness practices, such as meditation, deep breathing exercises, or mindful walks, into your daily routine. Being present and fully engaged in the moment can help you find greater clarity, focus, and appreciation for the present.

9. Pursue Creative Expression: Engage in creative pursuits that allow you to express yourself and explore your inner world. This could involve writing, painting, playing music, or any other form of artistic expression that resonates with you.

10. Reflect on Your Legacy: Consider the impact you want to have and the legacy you hope to leave behind. This could involve setting long-term goals, mentoring others, or contributing to causes that will have a lasting positive influence on the world around you.

Remember, finding purpose and meaning is a deeply personal journey, and what resonates with one individual may differ from another. The key is to approach these exercises with an open mind, a willingness to explore, and a commitment to living a life that aligns with your deepest values and aspirations.

**Here are 20 questions that serve as a checklist to measure progress on the topic of living a purpose life as well as provide pointers:**

1. What brings you the deepest sense of fulfilment and meaning?

This question prompts reflection on activities, relationships, or pursuits that provide a profound sense of purpose. For example, Srinivas, a software engineer, found that mentoring young coders gave her life deeper meaning than her day-to-day work. Ved, a retiree, discovered fulfilment in volunteering at a local animal shelter.

Neuroscience research by Ishizu & Zeki (2014) shows that when people describe their deepest sources of meaning, there's increased activity in the brain's reward and decision-making regions. This suggests that engaging in meaningful activities isn't just emotionally satisfying, but also neurologically rewarding.

2. What values or principles guide your life decisions?

This question encourages examination of core beliefs that shape one's choices and behaviors. For instance, Vidya, an environmental activist, bases her decisions on sustainability and ecological responsibility. Mayank, a teacher, prioritizes integrity and compassion in his interactions with students and colleagues.

Neurologically, individuals with a stronger sense of purpose show increased activity in the prefrontal cortex, which is involved in decision-making, planning, and goal-directed behavior (Sumner et al., 2016). This suggests that having clear guiding principles can enhance our ability to make decisions aligned with our values and long-term goals.

3. How can you positively impact the lives of others?

This question focuses on altruism and social contribution. Examples might include Lavanya, a nurse who finds purpose in providing compassionate care to patients, or Pankaj, who started a community garden to promote healthy eating and community bonding.

Engaging in purposeful activities, especially those that benefit others, has been associated with increased levels of dopamine, a neurotransmitter linked to motivation and reward (Volkow et al., 2011). This biological response may explain why acts of kindness and service often feel rewarding and motivating.

4. What legacy do you hope to leave behind?

This question encourages long-term thinking about one's impact. For example, Ananya, a climate scientist, hopes her research will contribute to sustainable environmental policies. Ramnath, a father, focuses on instilling strong values in his children as his legacy.

Studies show that having a sense of purpose, including thinking about one's legacy, is linked to better physical and mental health, increased resilience, and even longevity (Hill & Turiano, 2014; Kim et al., 2020).

5. What are your unique talents and how can you use them to make a difference?

This question helps identify personal strengths and their potential applications. For instance, Siddharth, an artist, uses his talent to create public murals that brighten urban spaces and spark community conversations.

Using one's talents purposefully can activate the brain's reward pathways, potentially increasing motivation and satisfaction (Kringelbach & Berridge, 2009).

6. How can you cultivate more gratitude and appreciation for life?

This question focuses on developing a positive mindset. Rana, a busy executive, started a daily gratitude journal, noting three things she's thankful for each day. Kashyap practices mindful appreciation during his morning walks.

Cultivating gratitude and savoring positive experiences has been shown to activate the brain's reward pathways and increase well-being (Kringelbach & Berridge, 2009).

7. What brings you a sense of awe and wonder?

This question encourages seeking out experiences that inspire amazement. For some, like amateur astronomer Keith, it might be stargazing. For others, like hiker Salil, it's experiencing nature's grandeur.

Experiences of awe can lead to increased activity in brain regions associated with social emotion and prosocial behavior, potentially contributing to a sense of connection and purpose.

8. How can you live more authentically, in alignment with your true self?

This question promotes self-reflection and honesty. For example, Anand left a high-paying but unfulfilling corporate job to pursue his passion for teaching.

Living authentically can reduce cognitive dissonance and stress, potentially leading to improved mental health and a stronger sense of purpose.

9. What relationships or connections are most important to you?

This question highlights the role of social bonds in finding purpose. For many, like grandmother Kalpana, family relationships are central. For others, like community organizer Raj, it's the connections formed through shared causes.

Strong social connections are associated with increased activity in the brain's reward centers and improved overall well-being.

10. How can you contribute to making the world a better place?

This question encourages thinking beyond personal interests. Examples include Yuvraj, who organizes beach clean-ups, or Ramanujam, who develops assistive technologies for people with disabilities.

Contributing to societal good can activate the brain's reward systems, potentially reinforcing altruistic behaviors and increasing sense of purpose.

11. What lifelong dreams or goals inspire you to keep growing?

This question promotes continuous personal development. For instance, Anamika dreams of writing a novel, while Manoj aspires to run a marathon in every continent.

Setting and pursuing goals can increase activity in the prefrontal cortex, enhancing motivation and decision-making abilities (Sumner et al., 2016).

12. How can you find more balance and inner peace in your life?

This question addresses mental well-being. Examples include Kamal practicing daily meditation, or Nadia setting clear work-life boundaries.

Practices that promote inner peace, like meditation, have been shown to affect brain structure and function, potentially improving emotional regulation and reducing stress.

13. What brings you a sense of purpose during challenging times?

This question explores resilience. For some, like cancer survivor Amita, it's supporting others facing similar challenges. For others, like laid-off worker Binod, it's using the setback as an opportunity to pursue a long-held dream.

Having a sense of purpose during difficulties is associated with increased resilience and better mental health outcomes (Hill & Turiano, 2014).

14. How can you live with more compassion and kindness towards others?

This question promotes empathy and altruism. Examples include Aisha volunteering at a homeless shelter, or Prabhat making a conscious effort to perform daily acts of kindness.

Compassionate actions can stimulate the release of oxytocin, often called the "bonding hormone," which can enhance feelings of connection and well-being.

15. What gives your life a sense of deeper meaning beyond material possessions?

This question encourages looking beyond materialism. For instance, Anita finds meaning in creating art, while Shravan finds it in his spiritual practice.

Engaging in meaningful non-material pursuits can activate reward centers in the brain, potentially providing a more sustainable source of satisfaction than material acquisitions.

16. How can you continue learning and expanding your knowledge?

This question promotes lifelong learning. Examples include retired engineer Mohan taking online courses in philosophy, or young professional Ayush learning a new language.

Continuous learning can promote neuroplasticity, potentially improving cognitive function and providing a sense of growth and purpose.

17. What beliefs or philosophies resonate with you most deeply?

This question explores personal worldviews. For some, like environmentalist Maya, it's deep ecology. For others, like teacher Kirat, it's humanistic education philosophy.

Aligning one's actions with deeply held beliefs can increase activity in the brain's reward and decision-making regions (Ishizu & Zeki, 2014).

18. How can you live more mindfully and fully present in each moment?

This question promotes mindfulness. Examples include lawyer Rohan practicing mindful eating, or bus driver Shah focusing fully on each passenger interaction.

Mindfulness practices have been shown to affect brain structure and function, potentially improving attention, emotional regulation, and overall well-being.

19. What are you most passionate about, and how can you pursue that passion?

This question encourages following one's interests. For instance, hobby photographer Diana turned her passion into a second career, while history buff Keerthi started a popular podcast about local legends.

Engaging in passionate pursuits can increase dopamine levels, enhancing motivation and satisfaction (Volkow et al., 2011).

20. How can you find more joy and appreciation in the simple pleasures of life?

This question promotes savoring everyday experiences. Examples include Tina taking time to enjoy her morning coffee, or gardener Ananth delighting in the growth of his plants.

Savoring positive experiences, even small ones, has been shown to activate the brain's reward pathways and increase well-being (Kringelbach & Berridge, 2009).

These questions, supported by neuroscience research, provide a comprehensive framework for exploring and clarifying one's purpose in life. By regularly reflecting on these areas, individuals can potentially enhance their sense of meaning, improve their well-being, and lead more fulfilling lives. By reflecting on these questions and considering the relevant research, individuals may gain deeper insights into their personal purpose and how to live a more meaningful and fulfilling life.

**List of neuroscience topics and concepts cited in Chapter 12: Purpose and a reason for a meaningful life:**

1. Activation of blissful brain states associated with realizing one's deepest purpose.

2. Enhancement of psychological wellbeing correlated with discovering personal meaning.

3. Increased activity in brain's reward and decision-making regions when describing sources of meaning (Ishizu & Zeki, 2014).

4. Heightened activity in the prefrontal cortex for individuals with a stronger sense of purpose (Sumner et al., 2016)

 - Associated with improved decision-making, planning, and goal-directed behavior

5. Increased dopamine levels linked to engaging in purposeful activities, especially those benefiting others (Volkow et al., 2011).

6. Activation of brain's reward pathways when using one's talents purposefully (Kringelbach & Berridge, 2009).

7. Stimulation of brain's reward pathways through gratitude and savoring positive experiences.

8. Increased activity in brain regions associated with social emotion and prosocial behavior during experiences of awe.

9. Activation of brain's reward centers associated with strong social connections.

10. Enhanced activity in the prefrontal cortex linked to setting and pursuing goals.

11. Changes in brain structure and function associated with practices promoting inner peace (e.g., meditation).

12. Release of oxytocin (the "bonding hormone") stimulated by compassionate actions.

13. Promotion of neuroplasticity through continuous learning.

14. Impact of mindfulness practices on brain structure and function.

- Potential improvements in attention, emotional regulation, and overall well-being.

15. Increased dopamine levels associated with engaging in passionate pursuits.

## Chapter 13
## Believing in Yourself: The Journey to Confidence and Success

Having self-belief is one of the most important things in life. When you truly believe in yourself, a whole new world opens up. You gain the confidence to chase your dreams, take on new challenges, and bounce back from setbacks stronger than before. But developing true, lasting self-belief is not always easy. It's a journey filled with ups and downs. This note is to inspire and guide you along that journey.

What is self-belief? It's having an unshakeable faith in your abilities, your worth, and your potential as a human being. With self-belief, you operate from a place of "I can" rather than "I can't." You see obstacles as opportunities rather than dead-ends. You bounce back from failures because you know they are temporary setbacks, not permanent condemnations of who you are.

The impact of strong self-belief cannot be overstated. Research shows it is linked to higher achievement, better physical and mental health, more satisfying relationships, and greater overall life satisfaction. A study of 33,000 people across more than 30 countries found that those with high self-belief were more successful in their careers and reported greater happiness.

Those without self-belief often live life playing it safe, afraid to step out of their comfort zones. They let doubts and fears call the shots, missing out on incredible opportunities as a result. Low self-belief also makes it much harder to recover from setbacks and failures. One could get stuck in a cycle of self-doubt and negative thinking that perpetuates itself.

But don't worry, self-belief is not something you either have or don't have - it's a skill that can be developed and strengthened over time. Here are some inspiring stories and strategies to help light that inner fire:

Real-Life Examples

Seema was in her 40s, stuck in a dead-end job she hated. For years, she dreamed of starting her own business but never believed she could do it. "Who am I to think I could be an entrepreneur?" she thought. One day, after being passed over for a promotion, something clicked. Anna realized her self-doubt was holding her back from achieving her dreams. She started taking evening classes, joined networking groups, and got a small business loan. Two years later, Anna's business is thriving and she's never been happier or more fulfilled. The only thing holding her back before was her own self-belief.

Twelve-year-old Virat struggled with severe dyslexia, barely getting pass grades at school. Teachers labeled him lazy or unintelligent. Virat started believing their negative projections and gave up, thinking success was impossible for him. However, his parents never lost faith in his abilities. They surrounded him with love, worked on building his confidence, and got him special tutoring. Virat persevered and ended up getting stellar grades, graduating at the top of his class. He went on to earn multiple degrees and now runs a successful technology company. If he had continued believing those hurtful labels, his full potential would have stayed buried.

Strategies for Building Self-Belief

Affirmations - These are short, powerful statements that reprogram your conscious and unconscious mind. Examples: "I am capable of great things," "I approve of myself," "I overcome obstacles with ease." Neuroscience shows that affirmations can literally begin reshaping your brain over time. Say them aloud daily while looking in the mirror.

Visualization - World-class athletes use visualization to boost self-belief and performance. See yourself calmly achieving your goals and overcoming any challenges through vivid mental images. This activates the same brain patterns as actually doing the thing.

Progress Logs - Each day, write down 3 wins from the day - no matter how small. Write it down and feel accomplished. Over time, this trains your brain to focus on what went well instead of the negatives.

Challenge Limiting Beliefs - Identify irrational, self-limiting beliefs like "I'm not good enough" or "I'll never be able to do that." Consciously challenge and replace them with more empowering beliefs.

Affirmative Friends - Spend more time with those who support, encourage and believe in you. Limit negative voices that reinforce doubt and self-criticism. You are the company you keep.

Building self-belief is a process. It takes daily practice and commitment. But the payoffs in confidence, resilience and fulfilment are immense and life-changing. No matter your past or current circumstances, you have an incredible reserve of untapped potential within you. Believe in yourself and you can achieve anything you put your heart and mind towards. I hope these words have sparked or reinforced that belief within you.

## Checklist: 10 Lessons for Developing Consistent, Strong Self-Belief

1. Practice Positive Self-Talk

The voice in your head shapes your reality. Neuroscience shows the brain literally changes based on the thoughts you repeat. Make a habit of counteracting negative self-talk with positive affirmations like "I am capable" or "I can do this." Over time, this rewires the brain for confidence.

2. Visualize Success

Elite athletes visualize winning before every performance. This activates the same brain patterns as actually doing the skill. Spend 5-10 minutes daily vividly picturing yourself succeeding at your goals. It builds pathways of belief.

3. Keep a Win Journal

Each day, write down 3 small wins - no matter how minor. This trains your brain to register accomplishments rather than dwelling on failures or negatives. Over time, it builds an achievement-focused mindset.

### 4. Face Fears Gradually

Approach things you fear in small, progressive steps. As the brain sees you conquering small challenges successfully, it develops the belief that you can handle bigger ones too. This is exposure therapy in action.

### 5. Celebrate Small Wins

The brain gets hooked on small rewards. Treat yourself (in a small way) for each accomplishment or self-belief milestone. This positive reinforcement makes the brain crave repeating that belief-building behavior.

### 6. Find Belief Buddies

Limit exposure to negative people who reinforce self-doubt. Actively seek out those who encourage and believe in you. Confidence and belief are "contagious" on a neurological level.

### 7. Act "As If"

Take on the body language, thought patterns and behaviors of a supremely confident person, even before fully believing it. This "faking it" helps reprogram the nervous system for authentic belief.

### 8. Study Role Models

Find people you admire who exude self-belief. Study how they carry themselves, talk, and make decisions from that grounded place. Model what resonates to accelerate your own transformation.

9. Practice Self-Acceptance

Self-belief starts with self-acceptance. Make an active effort to remove any "conditions" you put on your self-worth. You have value simply for being human - believe that fully.

10. Be Patient and Persistent

Building deep-rooted self-belief takes time and conscious effort. Stick with belief-boosting practices even after lapses or setbacks. Like any neural rewiring, it's a gradual process that compounds over time.

Here are 20 questions that encourage self-reflection and building self-belief and confidence:

1. What are three of my biggest strengths or positive qualities?

This question encourages self-awareness and appreciation. Recognizing your strengths boosts confidence and helps you leverage these qualities in various aspects of life. It shifts focus from weaknesses to positive attributes, fostering a more balanced self-image and increased self-esteem.

2. What past accomplishments am I most proud of?

Reflecting on past achievements reinforces self-belief and motivation. It serves as a reminder of your capabilities and perseverance. This question helps build confidence by highlighting your ability to overcome challenges and succeed, providing encouragement for future endeavors.

3. How do my negative thoughts tend to distort reality?

This question promotes awareness of cognitive distortions. By identifying patterns of negative thinking, you can challenge and reframe these thoughts. This awareness is crucial for developing a more realistic and balanced perspective, leading to improved mental health and self-confidence.

4. Who are people in my life who believe in me unconditionally?

Recognizing your support system reinforces your sense of worth and belonging. It reminds you that you're valued and capable, even when self-doubt creeps in. This question highlights the importance of nurturing relationships that bolster your self-belief and provide emotional support.

5. What body language habits project confidence versus doubt?

Understanding your non-verbal communication helps you present yourself more confidently. This awareness allows you to make conscious changes to your body language, potentially influencing both how others perceive you and how you feel about yourself. It's a practical step towards embodying confidence.

6. What brave things have I done that defied my fears?

Recalling past acts of courage reinforces your ability to face challenges. This question reminds you of your inner strength and resilience. It provides evidence of your capability to overcome fears, boosting confidence when confronting new obstacles.

7. How do I typically react or cope after failures or setbacks?

Understanding your response to challenges is crucial for developing resilience. This question helps identify healthy and unhealthy coping mechanisms. By recognizing your patterns, you can cultivate more effective strategies for bouncing back from setbacks, fostering long-term emotional well-being.

8. What limiting beliefs do I have about my capabilities?

Identifying limiting beliefs is the first step to challenging and changing them. This question prompts you to examine self-imposed restrictions on your potential. Recognizing these beliefs allows you to question their validity and replace them with more empowering thoughts.

9. How have I unconsciously self-sabotaged in the past?

Recognizing self-sabotaging behaviors helps break negative patterns. This question encourages honest self-reflection on actions that may be holding you back. By identifying these behaviors, you can make conscious efforts to change them, paving the way for personal growth and success.

10. What role models exemplify unshakable self-belief to me?

Identifying inspiring figures provides concrete examples of self-belief in action. This question helps you visualize what unwavering confidence looks like, offering aspirational models. It can motivate you to cultivate similar qualities and provide guidance on how to embody self-belief.

11. What goals or dreams excite me yet also feel doubtful about achieving?

This question encourages you to confront both your aspirations and fears. It helps identify areas where self-doubt may be holding you back from pursuing your dreams. Recognizing these conflicting feelings is the first step towards overcoming fears and taking action towards your goals.

12. How does my negative self-talk typically sound? What would I tell a friend instead?

This question highlights the disparity between how we treat ourselves and others. It encourages self-compassion by prompting you to extend the same kindness to yourself that you would to a friend. This awareness can help transform harsh self-criticism into supportive self-talk.

13. In what areas of my life do I feel most confident? How can I amplify that?

Identifying areas of confidence provides a foundation for growth. This question helps you recognize your strengths and consider how to apply them more broadly. By amplifying existing confidence, you can gradually increase self-assurance in other areas of life.

14. What personal values make me feel proud and empowered when living by them?

Connecting with your values strengthens your sense of self and purpose. This question helps you identify principles that guide your actions and decisions. Living in alignment with these values can boost self-esteem and provide a sense of authenticity and empowerment.

15. How might acting "as if" I'm supremely confident slowly make it feel natural?

This question introduces the concept of 'believe in it till you make it.' It encourages experimenting with confident behavior, even if it feels unnatural at first. This practice can help build real confidence over time, as your actions and self-perception gradually align.

16. What are three small wins or accomplishments I can celebrate from this week?

Recognizing daily achievements fosters a positive mindset and builds self-esteem. This question encourages you to acknowledge and celebrate small successes, which often go unnoticed. Regular practice of this can cultivate a habit of self-appreciation and boost overall confidence.

17. How might visualizing success and achievement rewire my brain over time?

This question introduces the power of mental rehearsal. Visualizing success can create new neural pathways, making achievement feel more attainable. This practice can boost confidence, reduce anxiety, and improve performance in various areas of life.

18. What self-care practices could boost my self-worth and self-acceptance?

Prioritizing self-care reinforces the belief that you're worthy of care and attention. This question encourages identifying practices that nurture your physical, emotional, and mental well-being. Regular self-care can significantly improve self-worth, reducing stress and enhancing overall life satisfaction.

19. How have my beliefs limited me in the past? How might new beliefs unlock potential?

This question promotes awareness of how beliefs shape experiences and opportunities. It encourages examining past limitations and considering how changing your mindset could open new possibilities. This reflection can motivate personal growth and the pursuit of previously dismissed opportunities.

20. On a scale of 1-10, how would I rate my current level of self-belief? Why?

This question provides a concrete assessment of your current self-belief. It encourages honest reflection on your confidence levels and the reasons behind them. This awareness serves as a starting point for improvement, helping you identify areas that need attention and celebrate progress made.

**List of the neuroscience topics and research cited in Chapter 13: Believing in Yourself: The Journey to Confidence and Success**

1. Research on self-belief: A study of 33,000 people across more than 30 countries found that those with high self-belief were more successful in their careers and reported greater happiness.

2. Affirmations and brain reshaping: Neuroscience shows that affirmations can literally begin reshaping your brain over time.

3. Visualization and brain patterns: Visualization activates the same brain patterns as actually performing an action.

4. Neuroplasticity and thought patterns: The brain literally changes based on the thoughts you repeat.

5. Exposure therapy: As the brain sees you conquering small challenges successfully, it develops the belief that you can handle bigger ones.

6. Reward system in the brain: The brain gets hooked on small rewards, which can be used to reinforce belief-building behaviors.

7. Social influence on the brain: Confidence and belief are described as "contagious" on a neurological level.

8. Body language and the nervous system: Taking on the body language of a confident person can help reprogram the nervous system for authentic belief.

9. Neural rewiring: Building deep-rooted self-belief is described as a gradual process of neural rewiring that compounds over time.

# Chapter 14
# The transformative power of Meditation

I want to share something truly life-changing with you today. It's a simple practice that has been around for centuries, yet its power is often overlooked in our fast-paced modern world. I'm talking about meditation – a profound journey inwards that can transform your life in ways you never imagined.

At its core, meditation is about cultivating present moment awareness. It's about quieting the constant chatter of the mind and simply being. In doing so, we create space for clarity, insight, and a deeper connection with ourselves and the world around us.

It is common to think, "But I've tried meditation, and my mind just won't stop racing." This happens to everyone initially. The idea of sitting still and doing "nothing" can seem daunting, even counterintuitive in our productivity-obsessed culture. But that's precisely why meditation is so powerful – it teaches us to embrace the present moment, without judgment or resistance.

Through regular practice, you'll begin to notice a profound shift in your perspective. The worries and anxieties that once consumed you will start to lose their grip. You'll find yourself responding to life's challenges with greater equanimity and wisdom.

Let me share a personal story that illustrates the transformative power of meditation. A few years ago, I was going through a particularly challenging time in my life. Work was overwhelming, relationships were strained, and I felt like I was drowning in a sea of stress. That's when a friend suggested I try meditation.

At first, I was skeptical. How could something as simple as sitting and breathing possibly make a difference? But I was desperate, so I gave it a shot.

Within a few weeks of regular practice, I noticed a subtle shift in my perspective. I was more present, more patient, and better able to separate my sense of self from the endless stream of thoughts and emotions. It was as if a weight had been lifted from my shoulders.

But the real magic happened when I faced a major setback at work. In the past, such an event would have sent me into a tailspin of anxiety and self-doubt. But this time, something was different. I could observe my thoughts and emotions with a newfound sense of detachment. I could see the situation for what it was – a temporary challenge, not a life-defining catastrophe.

This clarity allowed me to respond with wisdom and grace, rather than react with fear and frustration. I was able to navigate the situation with a level head and find a solution that not only resolved the immediate issue but also set me on a path toward greater professional growth and fulfillment.

That's the power of meditation – it gives you the ability to step back from the constant chatter of the mind and see things for what they truly are. It cultivates a sense of inner peace and resilience that allows you to navigate life's challenges with grace and wisdom.

But the benefits of meditation go far beyond just stress reduction and improved decision-making. Regular practice has been shown to have profound effects on our physical and mental well-being.

Neuroscience research has revealed that meditation can actually restructure the brain, increasing gray matter density in areas associated with emotional regulation, memory, and decision-making. It can also reduce activity in the amygdala, the brain's "fear center," leading to decreased anxiety and improved emotional stability.

Perhaps most significantly, meditation has been shown to increase activity in the prefrontal cortex, the part of the brain responsible for higher-order thinking, planning, and self-regulation. This means that regular practice can enhance our ability to focus, think critically, and make wise choices – essential skills in our increasingly complex world.

Consider the case of Kalpana, a busy mom juggling the demands of work, family, and a never-ending to-do list. Kalpana had always been a worrier, constantly ruminating over the past and fretting about the future. It wasn't until she stumbled upon a meditation app that she found a way to quiet her restless mind.

At first, Kalpana struggled to sit still for more than a few minutes. Her mind would race from one thought to the next, caught up in a whirlwind of mental chatter. But she persisted, committing to just 10 minutes of practice each day.

Over time, Kalpana noticed a remarkable shift. She found herself feeling calmer and more centered, even in the midst of chaos. She was better able to stay present with her children, savoring the fleeting moments of their childhood. And when challenges arose, she could respond with clarity and wisdom, rather than getting swept away by fear and anxiety.

Kalpana's story is just one of countless examples of the transformative power of meditation. From improved focus and concentration to enhanced emotional intelligence and overall well-being, the benefits of this simple practice are truly profound.

Meditation is something anyone can do, anytime, anywhere. You don't need any special equipment or fancy retreats. All you need is a willingness to sit quietly and tune into the present moment.

Of course, like anything worthwhile, meditation takes practice and patience. It's not about achieving a state of perpetual bliss or emptying your mind of all thoughts (that's practically impossible!). It's about cultivating a gentle, non-judgmental awareness of whatever arises in the present moment.

So, if you find your mind wandering during meditation, don't beat yourself up. Simply acknowledge the distraction, and gently bring your attention back to your breath. Remember, the practice itself is the goal – not some idealized state of perfect stillness.

As you deepen your practice, you'll begin to notice subtle shifts in your perspective and way of being. You'll find yourself responding to life's challenges with greater equanimity and wisdom. You'll cultivate a deeper sense of compassion and understanding, not just for others, but for yourself as well.

And perhaps most importantly, you'll discover the true gift of meditation – a profound connection with the present moment, the only reality we ever truly have.

I encourage you to embark on this journey inwards. It may seem daunting at first, the rewards are beyond measure. Whether you're seeking stress relief, clarity of mind, or a deeper sense of meaning and purpose, meditation has the power to transform your life in ways you never imagined.

So take a deep breath, close your eyes, and simply be. The journey awaits.

**Here is a checklist of 10 actionable items to help develop a meditative state of mind with examples:**

1. Start small. Don't overwhelm yourself by trying to meditate for hours right away. Begin with just 5-10 minutes per day and gradually increase over time. For example, you could set a timer for 5 minutes in the morning while sipping your coffee or tea.

2. Find a quiet space. While not absolutely necessary, having a designated meditation space can help signal to your brain that it's time to be present. This could be a peaceful corner of your living room, a spot in your backyard, or even your parked car before work.

3. Get comfortable. Wearing loose, comfortable clothing and finding a position that doesn't cause strain or distraction is important. You can sit cross-legged, kneel, or simply sit upright in a chair. Use props like cushions or blankets to support your body as needed.

4. Focus on your breath. A common meditation technique is to simply focus on the sensation of your breath moving in and out. When your mind wanders,

gently return your attention to your inhales and exhales. You can mentally note "inhale," "exhale" to help anchor your awareness.

5. Try a guided meditation. If you're struggling to stay present, a guided meditation app or recording can help by providing a teacher's voice to focus on. It removes the need to self-guide and can make meditation feel more accessible.

6. Notice sensations. Another method is to simply notice the physical sensations you're experiencing like the feeling of your feet on the floor, your hands resting on your lap, or any sounds, smells, or breezes. Tune into the present through your senses.

7. Move your meditation. Meditative practices don't have to be static. Try a walking meditation by slowing your pace and focusing fully on the experience, or do gentle, mindful movements like qigong or simple stretches.

8. Don't judge wandering thoughts. When your mind inevitably wanders during meditation, don't judge or berate yourself. Gently acknowledge the thought and let it go, returning to your point of focus. Wandering is normal and natural.

9. Find a community. Joining a meditation group, either online or in-person, can provide a shared experience and

accountability. You can learn from others and know you aren't alone in your practice.

10. Be patient and consistent. Meditation is simple but not always easy. Benefits come with regular, sustained practice over time. Don't get discouraged. Celebrate your daily efforts, no matter how small, and be kind to yourself throughout the process.

**Here is a list of 20 reflective questions that serve as a check for the strength of one's meditative practice, offer pointers for improvement, highlight potential benefits, and underscore the importance of meditation:**

1. How often do you find yourself feeling overwhelmed, stressed, or anxious in your daily life?

2. When was the last time you felt truly present and engaged in the current moment, without your mind wandering?

3. Do you find yourself frequently caught up in negative thought patterns or excessive worry about the past or future?

4. How well are you able to regulate and manage difficult emotions like anger, sadness or fear?

5. Do you struggle with insomnia, restlessness or an overly active mind at night?

6. When faced with challenges or setbacks, are you able to respond with wisdom and clarity rather than getting hijacked by your emotions?

7. How capable do you feel at truly listening to others without judgement or mental distraction?

8. Do you often find it difficult to make decisions or consistently follow through on your intentions?

9. How connected do you feel to the present moment and the simple joys of daily living?

10. When was the last time you felt a profound sense of peace, wholeness or spiritual connection?

11. How often do you take time to pause and check in with yourself during the day?

12. Are you able to maintain focus on tasks without getting easily distracted?

13. How well do you handle unexpected changes or disruptions to your plans?

14. Do you find yourself reacting impulsively in situations, or can you pause before responding?

15. How often do you experience a sense of gratitude and appreciation for the little things in life?

16. Are you able to observe your thoughts and emotions without getting caught up in them?

17. How comfortable are you with silence and being alone with your thoughts?

18. Do you have a regular time and place set aside for your meditation practice?

19. How often do you extend compassion to yourself, especially when you've made a mistake?

20. Can you easily let go of grudges or resentments, or do you tend to hold onto them?

These questions not only assess the current state of your meditation practice but also point to areas where you might be missing out on the benefits of a strong meditative mindset. They highlight the importance of meditation in cultivating emotional regulation, stress management, focus, compassion, and overall well-being. By reflecting on these questions, you can identify areas for growth and motivation to deepen your practice.

**List of neuroscience topics and research cited in Chapter 14: The transformative power of Meditation**

1. Restructuring of the brain through meditation
- Increased gray matter density in areas associated with:
    a. Emotional regulation
    b. Memory
    c. Decision-making

2. Reduced activity in the amygdala (the brain's "fear center") due to meditation
- Effects:
    a. Decreased anxiety
    b. Improved emotional stability

3. Increased activity in the prefrontal cortex from meditation
- Areas of impact:
    a. Higher-order thinking
    b. Planning
    c. Self-regulation
- Resulting benefits:
    a. Enhanced focus
    b. Improved critical thinking
    c. Better decision-making

# Chapter 15
# Coping with turbulent thoughts (inner violence)

We all experience turbulent, violent thoughts from time to time - harsh mental storms that can shake us to the core. These inner tempests of anxiety, anger, self-criticism and fear can wreak havoc on our peace of mind and wellbeing. Left unbridled, they can corrode our self-worth, cloud our judgment, and sabotage our ability to lead a fulfilling life.

But we are not powerless against these mental maelstroms. By understanding their origins and cultivating serene steadiness, we can navigate turbulence with grace. With gentle determination, we can quell inner violence and nurture the unshakable calm that allows our highest selves to flourish.

The Harmful Impact of Turbulent Thoughts

Our brains are hard-wired to reflexively react to perceived threats - whether physical dangers or intrusive thoughts. This instantaneous "fight-or-flight" response floods our body with stress hormones like cortisol and adrenaline, putting us in a state of high alert.

While this hypersensitivity aided our ancestors in evading predators, in our modern world it can be triggered by non-life-threatening stressors like money worries, conflict, or self-critical thoughts. When the brain's ancient alarm system gets stuck in the "on" position, it can have devastating effects:

Mental health consequences: Chronic negative thinking patterns activate the brain's "worry" centers like the amygdala, releasing a torrent of anxiety, rumination, and obsessive thoughts. This creates a vicious cycle, reinforcing pessimistic biases. Over time, it can contribute to clinical conditions like depression and addiction.

Physical toll: The cardiovascular, immune, and nervous systems go into overdrive when turbulent thoughts persistently provoke a stress response. This increases inflammation and vulnerability to illness like heart disease, diabetes, and chronic pain.

Relationships strained: In the grip of harsh inner commentary, we are more likely to lash out at loved ones, perceive negativity where there is none, isolate ourselves, and struggle with empathy.

Poor choices: When cortisol and adrenaline spike, the brain's executive centers that govern focus, decision making, and impulse control go offline. This materially impairs judgment, creativity, and quality of life.

As these examples illustrate, toxic thought patterns can sabotage our well-being on multiple levels - corroding us from within like acid dissolving metal if left to fester.

Attaining the Stillness of Calm Self-Mastery

While we cannot control turbulent thoughts from spontaneously arising, we can cultivate the presence and discipline to respond to them with level-headed wisdom. This self-regulation, enabled by the brain's prefrontal cortex, allows us to override destructive knee-jerk reactions with conscious choice.

When turbulence strikes, the prefrontal cortex is our voice of reason - helping us pause, objectively examine agitating thoughts, and reframe them in a more constructive light. Like a thermostat cooling a hot room, this higher cognition modulates the amygdala's fire, settling the mind into composure.

Crucially, when we create distance from negative thoughts instead of engaging them, we weaken the neural pathways that reinforce them. Over time, this starves toxic patterns and makes it easier for the prefrontal cortex to maintain dominion.

Training in secular meditation, mindfulness, and cognitive therapies can strengthen our ability to respond to turbulence with collected calm. By anchoring our attention in the present through concentrated breathing, we become less trapped by looping mental storms.

When we make mindful presence a habit, we more readily recognize when our narrative has taken a toxic turn. We can then consciously steer our thoughts, like a captain steadying a ship in rough waters, toward what spiritually nourishes us.

Stoic philosophy offers another powerful tool for coping with inner turbulence. By cultivating perspective, we can insulate ourselves from debilitating thought patterns rooted in catastrophizing, control dramas, and misplaced expectations.

The tenets of Stoicism teach us to focus solely on what we can control (our reactions) versus what we cannot (external events). This frees us from being consumed by situations beyond our influence, anchoring us in humble equanimity. It also underscores the empowering principle that while we cannot control every thought that arises, we can control how we respond.

Combined with steady mindful presence, reason, and willpower, the Stoic ideal of simplicity - discarding inessential wants in favor of fulfillment through virtue - offers profound insulation against mental restlessness. When our core sense of contentment stems from our values rather than circumstance, we become unshakable in the face of turbulence.

Other philosophies and faiths around the world have developed potent medicines for soothing storms of thought. Acceptance and surrender - hallmarks of major wisdom traditions of the world - steadfastly guide us away from futilely fighting what we cannot change, and back toward gratitude and trust in life's unfolding.

Ultimately, through regular practice, coping modalities like these become more than techniques - they instill a self-mastery that rewires our brains for equilibrium. Just as physical exercise strengthens muscles, mental exercise conditions the prefrontal cortex and other calm-inducing neural networks to automatically override reactivity with presence.

Slowly but surely, we tame the tyrant of inner violence and rediscover our core serenity amidst inevitable turbulence. Like still waters running deep beneath surface waves, we embody the unflappable calm of sages through all of life's changes.

Moving Forward with Patience and Self-Care

Becoming the master - rather than the victim - of inner turbulence takes immense patience, commitment and self-compassion. Given the brain's neuroplasticity, it's never too late to begin this journey, but it requires diligent practice and kindness toward ourselves.

Some turbulent thoughts will inevitably resurface despite our best efforts. When this happens, we must avoid compounding the situation by layering judgment atop self-criticism. With gentleness, we gently guide our mind away from punishing narratives and back toward presence.

Supportive outlets like journaling, therapy, and hiking offer powerful ways to process stormy mental weather in a productive manner. Confiding in loved ones, or speaking and writing our troubles provide additional catharsis.

It's also important to nurture the body. Turbulence takes a physical toll, requiring activities like yoga, massage, and adequate sleep to keep our vessels grounded and resilient. Eating nutritious foods prevents wild blood sugar fluctuations that exacerbate mood instability. Experimenting to find an optimal lifestyle balance is highly personal and takes patience.

Ultimately, a courageous spirit of curiosity and good humor will serve us best on this lifelong path of growth. We aren't striving for perpetual bliss so much as flexibility - equanimity in the midst of life's inevitable storms. With self-compassion and commitment, we gradually shed layers of inner violence and rediscover the pristine peace at our core. Each stumble is an opportunity to recalibrate and try again, without judgment. Each insight along the way deepens our embodiment of hard-won wisdom.

Like a tree weathering high winds, turbulence makes us more resilient over time. And with a foundation of calm self-mastery, our strength grows from within. So let us boldly face inner tumult not as a curse, but as a cathedral for the spirit - the fires that return us to the eternal stillness we've carried all along.

**Here are 10 practical, actionable items that can be easily incorporated into a daily routine to help cope with inner turbulence and minimize the impact of violent thoughts:**

1. Practice mindful breathing. When we're gripped by turbulent thoughts, consciously taking a few deep breaths can engage the brain's prefrontal cortex and calm the amygdala's "fight-or-flight" response. Breathe in through your nose to a count of 4, hold for 4, then exhale through pursed lips to a count of 6. This simple act reduces anxiety and restores equilibrium.

2. Keep a thought journal. Writing about intrusive thoughts in a personal notebook or online journal allows us to process them objectively. This activates the prefrontal cortex's reasoning and curbs the amygdala's reactivity. Over time, it weakens the neural pathways reinforcing negative thought patterns while strengthening positive ones.

3. Meditate daily. Neuroscience shows regular meditation, even 5-10 minutes per day, strengthens the brain's attentional control, emotional regulation, and ability to detach from rumination. It activates the insula and prefrontal cortex while cooling the amygdala's hair-trigger stress response.

4. Exercise regularly. Aerobic exercise releases mood-boosting endorphins while decreasing stress hormones

like cortisol. It stimulates neurogenesis in the hippocampus, fortifying the brain against depression and anxiety. Even walking for 30 minutes can provide substantial cognitive benefits.

5. Practice cognitive reframing. When turbulent thoughts arise, consciously reframe them in a more balanced, constructive light. This engages the prefrontal cortex, weakening the amygdala's threat response. For example, reframe "I'm a failure" as "I'm still learning, and struggles are temporary."

6. Schedule daily downtime. Build 30-60 minutes of personal time into your schedule to relax, unwind and recharge without stimulants like TV, social media or work. This calms the amygdala. Use this time for activities like meditation, yoga, reading or just being present.

7. Get adequate sleep. Quality sleep is crucial for the brain to rest and reset from emotional turbulence. Poor sleep amplifies negative thinking by impairing the prefrontal cortex's ability to regulate the amygdala. Strive for 7-9 hours per night.

8. Foster nurturing relationships. Strong social ties reduce feelings of loneliness and isolation that intensify negative thought loops. Oxytocin released through caring bonds has a calming effect on the amygdala while boosting the prefrontal cortex.

9. Spend time in nature. Being in green spaces soothes the brain by lowering blood pressure, heart rate, and stress hormones. The visual patterns of nature engage the brain's attention networks in a restorative way, quieting the amygdala's turmoil.

10. Practice self-compassion. Meeting our turbulent thoughts with kindness rather than harsh self-judgment prevents the amygdala from escalating into a vicious cycle. Self-compassion activates the brain's soothing capacities and reduces destructive rumination.

**Here are 20 self-reflective questions that can help assess one's level of inner calm, expertise in dealing with inner turbulence and violent thoughts:**

1. How often do I experience intense bouts of anger, anxiety or self-criticism throughout the day?

2. Do I have a regular meditation or mindfulness practice to cultivate present-moment awareness?

3. When turbulent thoughts arise, how quickly can I detach from them and let them pass without engaging?

4. Do I tend to catastrophize or blow things out of proportion when faced with challenges?

5. How well can I regulate my emotions and return to a state of calm after an upsetting event?

6. Do I have a support system of loved ones I can confide in when struggling with inner turmoil?

7. How much time do I spend ruminating or obsessing over past events I cannot change?

8. Do I have healthy outlets like exercise, journaling or creative pursuits to process difficult emotions?

9. How compassionately do I treat myself when experiencing setbacks or shortcomings?

10. Do I prioritize getting sufficient sleep and nutrition to support my emotional wellbeing?

11. How often do intrusive, negative thoughts prevent me from being fully present and engaged?

12. Do I have techniques like cognitive reframing to challenge irrational, self-destructive thought patterns?

13. How much control do I feel I have over my negative inner voice and its impact on my mood?

14. Do I have a sense of life purpose and core values that provide perspective during turbulence?

15. How comfortable am I simply allowing turbulent thoughts to arise and pass without judging them?

16. Do I make time for restorative activities like being in nature, yoga or reading inspiring texts?

17. How deeply have I explored the root causes and triggers of my most persistent inner storms?

18. Can I call upon feelings of faith, gratitude or acceptance when facing turbulence I cannot control?

19. How much have I learned from past experiences of navigating turmoil and finding my center?

20. Do I have a vision for my highest, most spiritually grounded self that inspires me through difficulty?

**List of neuroscience topics and research cited in Chapter 15: Coping with turbulent thoughts (inner violence):**

1. The brain's "fight-or-flight" response: This ancient survival mechanism can be triggered by non-life-threatening stressors in modern life, potentially leading to chronic stress.

2. Release of stress hormones: Cortisol and adrenaline flood the body during stress responses, putting us in a state of high alert that can be detrimental if prolonged.

3. Activation of brain's "worry" centers: Chronic negative thinking activates areas like the amygdala, potentially creating a vicious cycle of anxiety and rumination.

4. Impact of chronic negative thinking: Persistent negative thought patterns can reinforce pessimistic biases and contribute to clinical conditions like depression and addiction.

5. Role of the prefrontal cortex: This brain region helps override destructive knee-jerk reactions with conscious choices, allowing for more level-headed responses to turbulent thoughts.

6. Neural pathways reinforcing thought patterns: Creating distance from negative thoughts can weaken

the neural pathways that reinforce them, making it easier to maintain composure over time.

7. Effects of meditation and mindfulness: These practices can strengthen our ability to respond to turbulence with collected calm by anchoring our attention in the present.

8. Impact of stress on body systems: Chronic stress can increase inflammation and vulnerability to illnesses like heart disease and diabetes by putting various body systems into overdrive.

9. Impairment of executive functions: When stress hormones spike, brain areas governing focus and decision-making can go offline, materially impairing judgment and quality of life.

10. Brain's neuroplasticity: The brain's ability to change and adapt means it's never too late to begin the journey of mastering inner turbulence.

11. Strengthening calm-inducing neural networks: Regular mental exercises can condition the brain to automatically override reactivity with presence.

12. Effects of journaling: Writing about intrusive thoughts can help process them objectively, activating the prefrontal cortex's reasoning and curbing the amygdala's reactivity.

13. Neuroscience findings on meditation: Regular meditation has been shown to strengthen the brain's attentional control, emotional regulation, and ability to detach from rumination.

14. Exercise's role in mood: Aerobic exercise releases mood-boosting endorphins while decreasing stress hormones, providing cognitive benefits.

15. Exercise-induced neurogenesis: Regular physical activity stimulates the growth of new neurons in the hippocampus, potentially fortifying the brain against depression and anxiety.

16. Cognitive reframing's brain engagement: Consciously reframing turbulent thoughts in a more balanced light engages the prefrontal cortex, weakening the amygdala's threat response.

17. Importance of sleep: Quality sleep is crucial for the brain to reset from emotional turbulence, as poor sleep can amplify negative thinking by impairing the prefrontal cortex's regulatory abilities.

18. Oxytocin release through social bonds: Strong social ties can reduce feelings of loneliness and isolation by releasing oxytocin, which has a calming effect on the amygdala while boosting the prefrontal cortex.

19. Nature's impact on the brain: Spending time in green spaces can soothe the brain by lowering physiological stress markers and engaging attention networks in a restorative way.

20. Self-compassion's brain activation: Meeting turbulent thoughts with kindness activates the brain's soothing capacities and reduces destructive rumination, preventing the amygdala from escalating into a vicious cycle.

# Chapter 16
# Connecting with nature

This chapter has some thoughts on the profound benefits of connecting with nature. In our fast-paced, modern world, it's all too easy to become disconnected from the natural environment that nurtured and sustained humanity for millennia. This writing is a lovingly reminder that forging a bond with the great outdoors could be one of the most rewarding and healing things we can do for body, mind and spirit.

We all have experienced feeling overwhelmed and frazzled with all the stresses and frenzied pace of life. The good news is that engaging with nature has been proven through rigorous neuroscience research to be an antidote to that anxiety and mental cloudiness. Studies show that being immersed in green spaces like forests, parks or gardens actually alters our brain activity in remarkably positive ways.

A landmark study from Stanford got a lot of attention when it revealed that volunteers who went for a 90-minute walk through a natural environment showed decreased activity in their subgenual prefrontal cortex compared to those who walked through urban areas. This region of the brain is associated with repetitive, negative thoughts and is linked to depression and anxiety. The nature walkers also exhibited lower levels of rumination (obsessive thought patterns) as well as less anxiety overall.

Researchers concluded that the sights, sounds and smells of walking in a natural setting appeared to relax the areas of the brain involved with brooding and worry, while simultaneously engaging the regions tied to heightening our sense of calm. There's real, solid neurological data backing up what we may have intuited all along - that nature has the power to quiet our minds and soothe our psyches. That's an incredible gift in our turbocharged era of constant distraction and overstimulation.

And the benefits of nature go far beyond just dialing down anxiety and negativity. Research shows that immersion in outdoor environments cultivates a childlike sense of awe, curiosity and wonder that our high-tech modern lives often neglect. A University of California study using brain imaging found that when people viewed scenes depicting the raw beauty of nature, their anterior cingulate cortex and insula became highly engaged. This indicated strong feelings of admiration, with the cortex and insula firing up the neural pathways associated with feeling moved by something wondrous and beautiful.

The researchers concluded that exposure to natural splendor awakens our primal senses of awe and curiosity in a unique way that urban environments cannot. The authors noted how feeling a sense of awe toward something greater than ourselves - whether appreciating the cosmos, witnessing the birth of a child, or being humbled by the magnificence of a towering waterfall - may deepen our humility and make us feel part of something far larger and more meaningful.

Does this ring true for you? I suspect it does based on experiences in nature's grandeur. You might remember the times when during camping and hiking you felt awe, a childlike wonder and astonishment. For those transcendent moments, all the internal mental chatter and preoccupations ceased, and you were fully present, at peace in the sacred grandeur. An encounter with such staggering natural phenomena has a way of recalibrating our perspective and restoring our sense of curiosity about the world.

Or an evening spent on the beach at sunset, utterly entranced by the sublime, shifting colors splashed across the sky as the sun's rays danced off the rippling ocean waves? In those moments we feel purified, unburdened and at ease, as if our entire being is spiritually recharged by the magnificence surrounding us. Experiences of beauty and awe like that enliven our sense of curiosity like little else can.

As Harvard researchers found, "Awe is the ultimate temporary perspective shift." When we gaze upon something vastly larger than ourselves that transcends our ordinary frames of reference, it triggers a reaction of lapsed circumspection and renewed curiosity about the world around us. And the great outdoors is brimming with countless sources of awe-inspiring phenomena to awaken our wonder - from the dizzying cosmic grandeur of a starry night sky, to the complex micro-worlds thrumming with life in a patch of forest soil, to the raw power and primordial rhythms of the roiling sea.

Regularly tapping into that sense of awe and childlike fascination can be incredibly reinvigorating for our mental, emotional and spiritual health in a world that often leaves little room for mystery and present-moment awareness. Studies show it makes us feel more curious, ethical, and attuned to the reality that there are still vast mysteries in the cosmos left to explore. In short, reconnecting with the natural world rekindles our lapsed circumspection and reminds us of the magic around every corner if we just take the time to notice.

Beyond the emotional and existential dimensions, spending quality outdoor time comes with plenty of physical health dividends as well. Sunlight helps our bodies naturally synthesize vitamin D, a crucial hormone that majority of adults are deficient in. Vitamin D impacts gene expression in over a thousand different genes and plays a vital role in immune function, brain health, bone strength, cardiovascular wellness and many other biological processes. So getting outside for some sunshine is truly one of the simplest ways to fortify our health on a cellular level.

What's more, research indicates that the very act of walking among trees and plants exposes us to organic compounds and aromatic emissions that can improve our mental and physical condition in tangible ways. Many have experienced the reinvigorating feeling of breathing in the rich piney scents of a forest - that's no coincidence. Trees release phytoncides like alpha-pinene and deltaterpenes that when inhaled have been shown to reduce stress hormones like cortisol in the body. Forest air has also been found to boost levels of disease-fighting white blood cells and anti-cancer proteins. Some studies even suggest compounds released by trees could have anti-anxiety and anti-depressant-like effects on our psyche.

And of course, the physical activity involved in walking, hiking, swimming, climbing, cycling or just moving our bodies in outdoor green spaces provides a wealth of clinically-proven health benefits for everything from cardiovascular fitness and weight management to improving balance, endurance and strength as we age. Couple that with the mood-lifting psychological effects of scenery changes, direct sunlight exposure and breathing fresh air, and it's clear that immersing ourselves in nature is one of the most holistic things we can do to care for ourselves on every level.

The growing body of solid, peer-reviewed research is impossible to deny. Interacting with nature is not just a nice amenity, it's a vital necessity for our cognition, emotional regulation, spiritual nourishment and overall physiological wellbeing. Yet so many of us have become deeply disconnected from the very source that spawned us. Our tech-saturated lives are too often spent indoors, staring at screens and missing out on the profound therapeutic benefits of the living, breathing world that surrounds us.

Life gets hectic and modern obligations make it all too easy to deprive ourselves of nature's simple pleasures. This calls for being more intentional about regularly immersing yourself in green spaces and natural environments. It quite literally has the power to heal us - mind, body and soul. You absolutely deserve to experience the solace, wonder, rejuvenation and perspective-shifting awe that only Mother Nature can provide.

The sense of clarity, equanimity and inner stillness felt after spending time hiking, swimming or walking in nature is no fluke - it's our entire system being recalibrated and rebalanced by spending time in its native thriving state. Our anxieties and negativity temporarily dissolve, curiosities are piqued, and physical body is invigorated. We reconnect with what's real, what's essential. And those benefits linger long.

Making a concerted effort to build more of those revitalizing nature interludes into our weekly routines can be very rewarding. It could be as simple as taking a 30-minute stroll through a local park on a lunch break or finding a quiet trail to walk along a couple evenings per week. Maybe a habit of rising early to watch the sunrise and soak in those first soul-stirring moments of morning light filtering through the trees. Or a weekend hike to gaze out over a vast vista.

Keeping a nature journal can help sharpen observational skills and cement those mindful, unhurried moments into memory. Jotting down the little details we notice - the iridescent wings of a dragonfly hovering over a creek, the velvet softness of a moss.

**10 actionable items on harnessing the healing power of nature:**

1. Start a morning nature routine. Even just 5-10 minutes spent outside first thing can be incredibly grounding. Drink your coffee on the patio while listening to the birds wake up. Or take a short walk around the neighborhood and notice any changes in the trees, plants or animal life since the day before. This sets an intentional tone and allows you to feel connected to the natural cycles.

Example: Sara began walking her dog around the block each morning before work. She found the crisp air and greenery helped clear her mind after a night of restless sleep. The sights and sounds of nature eased her into her day in a calm, centered way.

2. Keep a nature journal. Documenting little observations strengthens your awareness. Jot down the first flower you see blooming each spring. Record the different bird calls you hear or make sketches of animal tracks. This mindful presence allows you to more fully appreciate the small wonders surrounding you.

Example: After moving to a new city, Varun started a nature journal to familiarize himself with the local flora and fauna. He found joy in watching the seasonal transitions and felt more connected to his new home environment.

3. Experience a body of water. Whether the ocean, a lake or just a serene river - being near bodies of water can induce a meditative state and promote healing. Schedule a weekend hike along a waterway or commit to monthly beach days. The gentle sounds of water have a calming effect on our psyche.

Example: Saurabh's favorite spot was a peaceful creek near his house. When he felt overwhelmed, he'd go sit by the babbling water, focus on his breaths and let his racing thoughts dissipate. The creek's soothing rhythm was incredibly restorative.

4. Stargaze on a clear night. Getting out at night and looking up at the vast, twinkling cosmos is remarkably humbling and induces awe. It shifts our perspective from the daily grind to an appreciation of our small place in the grand universe. Even just 10 minutes of stargazing can be phenomenally restorative.

Example: Every few weeks, Ram's family would pack some snacks and drive out to the countryside after dinner to stargaze and chart constellations. These nights sparked curiosity and were a treasured bonding experience.

5. Eat a meal outdoors. Whether a weekday breakfast on the patio or a weekend picnic lunch at a park, prioritize eating some meals surrounded by nature. The fresh air and natural ambiance cultivates a greater sense of presence, calm and gratitude.

Example: Hiresh had a habit of eating his mid-day meals at a shaded bench in the courtyard near his office. The outdoor setting was a peaceful reprieve, giving him an energized second-wind for the workday ahead.

6. Keep plants around your living spaces. Having living greenery like potted plants or even fresh-cut flowers has a tangible effect on well-being. Studies show indoor plants can boost mood, reduce stress and improve air quality. For a mood-lift, place plants in oft-frequented rooms.

Example: Jaya loved tending to her collection of household plants as a way to decompress after long days. The simple act of watering her green companions helped her feel more serene and grounded.

7. Take a working break in a green space. Rather than having coffee indoors, take your breaks in a garden, courtyard or the shade of a tree occasionally. The restorative effects of even brief doses of nature-exposure can enhance focus and creativity.

Example: After reading the benefits of nature breaks, the software firm Prasanth worked at designated an outdoor area with tables and planted trees for employees to enjoy breaks outside. He noticed an uptick in his own productivity after utilizing this green respite.

8. Do light exercises outdoors. Gentle movements like walking, yoga, tai chi or qigong become even more therapeutic when performed in nature's nurturing environs. The greenery, fresh air and shift in surroundings facilitate a meditative state.

Example: Every Saturday morning, Malvika's neighborhood yoga group would meet at the public garden to flow through an invigorating vinyasa routine. The beauty and sounds of the gardens always left her feeling more balanced.

9. Listen to natural soundscapes. If you can't regularly get outdoors, bring recordings of nature sounds indoors. The gentle ambience of ocean waves, rainfall, wind through trees or crackling fires can rapidly soothe our overstimulated minds.

Example: When Hiresh worked from home, he used a website of natural audio tracks to pipe soothing brook and birdsong atmospheres through his computer's speakers. It masked distracting noises and made his living room feel like an outdoor refuge.

10. Cultivate a window garden. For those without yards or gardens, use window planters to grow herbs, flowers or vegetables. Nurturing life helps us feel grounded while providing exposure to greenery. The acts of planting, tending and eventually harvesting can be incredibly rewarding.

Example: Living in an apartment, Anna found immense fulfillment in her diverse window garden of herbs, tomatoes and colorful flowers. She loved watching wildlife like birds visit her planter-boxes and seeing her efforts quite literally blossom.

**Here are 20 self-reflection questions to assess how effectively you are connecting with nature and to serve as a reminder:**

1. When was the last time you spent at least 30 minutes outdoors in a natural setting like a park, forest, beach or hiking trail?

2. Do you make it a habit to get outside for some portion of each day, even if just for a brief walk?

3. Can you recall the last time you felt a sense of awe or wonder at the beauty of nature?

4. How often do you intentionally unplug from devices and technology to be fully present in the outdoor world?

5. Do you have houseplants or fresh flowers indoors to bring nature's vitality inside?

6. When was the last time you paused to observe details in nature like clouds, trees budding, animal behaviors?

7. Do you feel a sense of peace, calm or rejuvenation after spending time outdoors?

8. How frequently do you engage in outdoor hobbies/activities like gardening, hiking, swimming, camping?

9. Do you have a favorite outdoor spot you return to regularly to connect with nature?

10. Are there any upcoming astronomical events like meteor showers or lunar eclipses you have noted to experience?

11. Do you open windows whenever possible to hear outdoor nature sounds and breathe fresh air?

12. How often do you dine or have leisurely meals in outdoor settings like your backyard or parks?

13. Do you have a nature hobby like bird watching, foraging or outdoor photography?

14. Have you noticed any seasonal transitions or cycles in your local plant/animal life recently?

15. How easy is it for you to take a break in a green space like a courtyard or garden during your workday?

16. Do you feel drawn to spend extended time in wilderness or remote natural areas when possible?

17. Can you remember any specific healing, grounding or meditative experiences you've had outdoors?

18. Are there any favorite nature books, writings or artworks that inspire your awe and curiosity?

19. Do you have plans to spend intentional time in nature on any upcoming days off or vacations?

20. What simple ways could you better integrate nature's calming presence into your daily routine?

**List of neuroscience topics and research cited in Chapter 16: Connecting with nature**

1. Stanford study on nature walks:

- 90-minute walks in natural environments decreased activity in the subgenual prefrontal cortex

- This brain region is associated with repetitive negative thoughts, depression, and anxiety

- Nature walkers showed lower levels of rumination and anxiety

2. Brain imaging study on viewing nature scenes:

- Conducted by the University of California

- Found increased engagement of the anterior cingulate cortex and insula

- These areas are associated with feelings of admiration and being moved by beauty

3. Harvard research on awe:

- Described awe as "the ultimate temporary perspective shift"

- Linked to changes in perception and curiosity

4. Studies on vitamin D synthesis:

- Sunlight exposure helps the body produce vitamin D

- Vitamin D impacts gene expression in over 1000 genes

- Plays a role in immune function, brain health, bone strength, and cardiovascular wellness

5. Research on phytoncides (organic compounds released by trees):

- Reduce stress hormones like cortisol in the body

- Boost levels of disease-fighting white blood cells and anti-cancer proteins

- May have anti-anxiety and anti-depressant-like effects

6. Studies on the effects of natural soundscapes:

- Gentle ambient sounds like ocean waves, rainfall, or wind through trees can soothe overstimulated minds

# Chapter 17
# Dealing with inner conflict

We all experience inner conflicts and struggles from time to time. It's part of being human. The constant push and pull between different desires, values, and impulses can leave us feeling drained, confused, and torn. But you don't have to be a prisoner to this inner tug-of-war. With some insightful perspectives and helpful practices, you can navigate through these choppy inner waters with more grace and self-compassion.

At the heart of many of our inner conflicts is the reality that the human brain is almost like a confederacy of semi-independent systems, each with its own goals and motivations. The prefrontal cortex, the CEO of the brain, tries to make wise long-term decisions aligned with our values and intentions. But it's constantly getting lobbied by other brain regions that just want immediate gratification or validation - the limbic system wants pleasurable feelings, the amygdala is primed for outrage and fear, and the brain's habit loops make us crave familiarity at the expense of growth.

No wonder we feel so divided at times. According to neuroscientist David Eagleman, "There's a civil war inside all of us - reason versus emotion, cool vs calculation versus desire." The good news is that with practice, you can get better at recognizing these different inner voices and cultivating more of what neuroscientist Daniel Siegel calls "integration" in the brain.

One key is to stop viewing your inner conflicts as a battle to be won, with one force needing to utterly conquer and silence the other. That black-and-white, adversarial framing only inflames the inner war. Instead, paradoxical as it sounds, you can learn to make room for multiple perspectives and drives within you - getting curious about them, seeing the reasons behind them, and looking for creative compromises.

For example, one woman I know struggled with procrastination at work, an inner conflict between the desire to work hard and succeed versus the urge to goof off and avoid difficult tasks. She could have berated herself as lazy or weak-willed, picking a clear side in her inner battle. But through self-exploration, she realized her procrastination was driven by perfectionistic thoughts ("If I can't do this perfectly, why bother?") and fears of burnout from her workaholic habits.

Understanding these root causes with compassion, she was able to make room for both her achievement drive and her needs for balance and self-care. She started prioritizing her tasks, setting firmer boundaries around working hours, and intentionally scheduling restorative breaks. Her inner conflict didn't magically vanish, but she found a sustainable path of travel.

Another common inner conflict arises when different parts of us have conflicting values or desires that feel sacred and inviolable. For instance, you may feel torn between nurturing independence in your children versus prioritizing family closeness and obedience. Or you may vacillate between wanting stability and comfort versus hungering for novelty, freedom, and adventure.

These intrinsic conflicts between core human needs don't have perfect resolutions, just dynamic calibrations based on context and priority. The paradoxical thinking that allows for "both/and" instead of "either/or" is invaluable here. As psychologist Paul T. P. Wong puts it, "The ability to transcend polarities and rise above adversity is the mark of a wise person."

Modern neuroscience strongly supports the notion that our sense of self is more of a running narrative than a monolithic, unchanging entity. In effect, we're a Work in Progress whose identity and values continually evolve through our choice of actions and interpretations. So when you feel torn by inner conflicts, see it as an opportunity for growth - a chance to reshape your neural pathways and update your personal narrative.

With a caring curiosity, you can ask yourself: What parts of me feel threatened or deprived when I make this choice? What dreams or aspirations would need to be sacrificed or amended here? How might I re-write this dilemma so that more of me feels honored and integrated?

Small mindset shifts like these can open up whole new vistas of possibility in seemingly hopeless conflicts. Often, the most exhausting inner battles come from our judgments about the conflicts themselves - our self-criticisms and unproductive resistance. By meeting your psyche's different facets with courageous compassion instead, we stand a better chance of achieving a harmonious inner state.

With patience and an open heart, we can make peace with our natural heterogeneity - the multiplicity of selves that make us gloriously human. Like a jazz improvisation, we can learn to harmonize the various melodies inside us in ever-shifting, transcendent ways.

**10 Actionable Items:**

1. Name your inner voices/selves and get to know their perspectives, needs, and motivations through reflective journaling.

2. Practice focusing your attention on just observing inner conflicts without judgment or struggle, like watching clouds passing through the sky.

3. When feeling torn, ask yourself "What small step could I take right now that would honor more of my different needs/values?"

4. Identify situations or relationships that trigger your strongest inner conflicts. How might you set better boundaries or change the conditions there?

5. Explore mindfulness practices like meditation that can increase self-awareness and promote neural integration.

6. Write out your personal narrative or life vision in a way that creatively incorporates more of your important identities and values.

7. Cultivate self-compassion by talking to yourself as you would a dear friend struggling with inner conflicts.

8. When paralyzed by a dilemma, temporarily remove "solution-finding" pressure by fully giving voice to all sides through journaling or discussion.

9. Study role models who seem to harmonize opposites with wisdom and grace. How might you embody those qualities?

10. Make a daily practice of looking for "both/and" solutions versus "either/or" choices in small situations to build your paradox-resolving skills.

**20 Self-Assessment Questions:**

1. What are the main inner voices or selves that you can identify within you, each with its own desires and concerns?

2. Which inner conflicts tend to cause you the most stress, self-judgment, and rumination?

3. How have you historically tried to resolve or cope with these intrinsic conflicts? What's worked well or become counterproductive?

4. To what degree do you approach your inner world with curiosity, compassion, and a desire to integrate versus an adversarial, winner-take-all mindset?

5. Can you think of any examples where you successfully found creative compromises or "both/and" solutions to inner conflicts?

6. Which relationships, environments, or thought patterns tend to inflame your inner conflicts and which tend to dampen or resolve them?

7. How might cultivating greater self-awareness and mindful presence help you navigate inner conflicts with more wisdom?

8. Do you find yourself overly attached to or invested in having a unified, conflict-free sense of self? How might you make room for multiplicity?

9. What personal qualities, values, or aspirations feel most sacred and inviolable, to the point of creating rigid inner standoffs?

10. Where in your life might you be able to practice allowing seeming opposites to co-exist in a paradoxical integration versus an either/or choice?

11. Can you think of role models who seem to navigate inner conflicts and polarities with grace? What can you learn from them?

12. How might journaling, contemplation, or discussions with others shed light on the deeper roots, histories, and unmet needs behind your inner conflicts?

13. To what degree are you practicing self-compassion versus harsh self-criticism in how you relate to your inner storms and divisions?

14. What small steps might you take to update your personal narrative in a way that feels more integrative of your different selves and values?

15. How might adjusting your external conditions (environments, habits, relationships) make certain inner conflicts feel less inflamed?

16. What mind-body practices might help quiet your inner chaos and promote greater neural integration?

17. Can you think of any inspiring metaphors that could help reframe how you experience inner conflicts (e.g. as an orchestra finding harmony)?

18. How might focusing more on "both/and" solutions be liberating or empowering versus feeling trapped in "either/or" dilemmas?

19. In terms of your most persistent inner battles, what's the cost of remaining stuck and what might be possible by finding new paths forward?

20. What's one small step you can take today to move in a more self-integrated, wise, and holistic direction with your inner experience?

I hope these perspectives and practices provide some solace and guidance as you compassionately work to harmonize your inner diversity.

# References to Neuroscience Topics in Chapter 17: Dealing with inner conflict

1. Structure and function of the prefrontal cortex:

The prefrontal cortex acts as the "CEO of the brain," making wise long-term decisions aligned with our values and intentions.

2. Role of the limbic system in pleasure and emotion:

The limbic system seeks immediate gratification and pleasurable feelings, often conflicting with long-term goals.

3. Function of the amygdala in fear and outrage responses:

The amygdala is primed for outrage and fear responses, potentially overriding more rational decision-making processes.

4. Brain's habit loops and their influence on behavior:

Habit loops in the brain make us crave familiarity, sometimes at the expense of personal growth and change.

5. Concept of the brain as a "confederacy of semi-independent systems":

The human brain operates like a confederacy of semi-independent systems, each with its own goals and motivations, leading to inner conflicts.

6. Neuroscientist David Eagleman's perspective on the "civil war" in our brains:

Eagleman describes an internal "civil war" between reason and emotion, cool calculation and desire, highlighting the complexity of human decision-making.

7. Neuroscientist Daniel Siegel's concept of "integration" in the brain:

Siegel's concept of "integration" represents a harmonious state where different parts of the brain work together effectively, reducing inner conflict.

8. Neural pathways and their reshaping through experience and choice:

Neural pathways can be reshaped through our experiences and choices, allowing us to actively work on resolving inner conflicts.

9. The brain's role in constructing a narrative sense of self:

Our sense of self is a running narrative constructed by the brain, rather than a fixed, unchanging entity, allowing for flexibility in identity.

10. Neural integration and its relationship to mindfulness practices:

Mindfulness practices can increase self-awareness and promote neural integration, helping to manage inner conflicts more effectively.

## Chapter 18
## Reflections of a Clear Mind: A Journey to Inner Serenity

In the hustle and bustle of our daily lives, we often find ourselves caught in a whirlwind of thoughts, emotions, and external stimuli. It's easy to feel overwhelmed, as if our minds are clouded by a thick fog that obscures our true selves. But within each of us lies a profound capacity for clarity, a state of mind as pure and reflective as a still mountain lake. This clarity is not a distant, unattainable goal but rather an inherent part of our nature, waiting to be revealed.

Imagine standing on a serene beach at dawn. As the first rays of sunlight dance across the water, you witness the ocean's surface transform from a turbulent expanse to a mirror-like calm. This natural phenomenon is a beautiful metaphor for the human mind. Just as the ocean's depths remain undisturbed even when its surface is agitated by winds and waves, your true essence remains untouched by the transient turmoil of everyday life.

Neuroscience has made remarkable strides in understanding this innate clarity. Researchers at the University of Wisconsin-Madison, led by Dr. Richard

Davidson, have conducted extensive studies on the brains of long-term meditators. They found that these individuals exhibit increased activity in the prefrontal cortex, the brain region associated with attention, emotional regulation, and self-awareness. This suggests that practices like mindfulness and meditation can help us access our natural state of mental clarity.

Consider the story of Sarah, a high-powered executive in New York City. Her days were a blur of meetings, deadlines, and digital notifications. She felt constantly on edge, her mind racing with worries about the future and regrets about the past. It wasn't until a health scare forced her to take a sabbatical that she discovered the power of a clear mind. During her time off, Sarah began practicing mindfulness meditation. At first, her thoughts were like a swarm of bees, but gradually, she learned to observe them without judgment. As the "dust" of her mental chatter settled, she found an underlying calmness that transformed her life. Upon returning to work, she was more focused, empathetic, and creative. Her newfound clarity didn't eliminate stress but allowed her to navigate it with grace.

The journey to mental clarity isn't always smooth. Picture a pond after a rainstorm. The water is murky, stirred up by the falling droplets. But given time, the sediment sinks, and the water clears, revealing the vibrant life beneath. Our minds are similar. Life's challenges – a difficult conversation, a professional setback, or personal loss – can stir up our mental waters. Yet, if we allow ourselves the space to process these experiences without clinging to them, clarity emerges.

This principle is beautifully illustrated in a study by neuroscientists at Harvard Medical School. They found that negative emotions activate the amygdala, our brain's "fight or flight" center. However, when participants were asked to label their emotions ("I feel angry"), activity shifted to the prefrontal cortex. This simple act of self-awareness helped regulate the emotional response, much like how naming the ripples on a pond's surface doesn't stop them but allows us to see through them more clearly.

The clear mind is not devoid of thought or emotion. Instead, it's a state where we're not controlled by them. It's akin to the vast blue sky that remains unchanged whether clouds pass or storms rage. This concept is central to many wisdom traditions and is now echoed by modern psychology. Dr. Daniel Siegel, a renowned psychiatrist, describes this as "mindsight" – the ability to observe our inner world with clarity and compassion.

Take the case of Parmanand, a schoolteacher in rural India. He worked in an area plagued by poverty and violence, conditions that often left him feeling hopeless and drained. A colleague introduced him to a local mindfulness group. Initially skeptical, Parmanand found that the practices helped him see his challenging circumstances with new eyes. He realized that while he couldn't control the external hardships, he could choose his response. His clear mind became a sanctuary, allowing him to be a pillar of strength for his students even on the toughest days.

The benefits of a clear mind extend beyond emotional resilience. A groundbreaking study from the University of California, Santa Barbara, showed that just two weeks of mindfulness training improved participants' working memory and GRE reading comprehension scores. The researchers attributed this to reduced mind-wandering. When our minds are clear, we're fully present, able to absorb and process information more effectively.

This clarity also enhances our relationships. Dr. John Gottman, famous for his work on marital stability, found that couples who practice mindfulness have greater empathy and conflict resolution skills. When we're not caught up in our own mental narratives, we can truly listen and connect with others. It's like two clear ponds reflecting each other, a communion of understanding.

However, in our technology-saturated world, finding this clarity can be challenging. Constant notifications, endless scrolling, and information overload can create a mental haze. But even here, neuroscience offers hope. A study from the University of California, Irvine, showed that after a mere 15-minute walk in nature, participants had reduced activity in the subgenual prefrontal cortex, a brain region active during rumination and negative moods. Nature, it seems, has a unique ability to clear our mental cobwebs.

As we conclude this journey through the reflections of a clear mind, remember that this clarity is not a distant shore but the very ground you stand on. It's the blue sky behind the clouds, the stillness beneath the waves. Every moment offers an invitation to return to this natural state.

In the words of the great Zen master Thich Nhat Hanh, "The present moment is filled with joy and happiness. If you are attentive, you will see it." This is the gift of a clear mind - the ability to see the joy inherent in each moment, to respond to life with wisdom rather than reaction, and to reflect the world with the compassionate, unbiased gaze of your true nature.

As you move forward, carry this understanding with you. In the midst of life's storms, remember the calm depths within. In the face of confusion, trust in the clarity that is inherent in your mind. And in every interaction, let your clear mind reflect the boundless sky of human potential.

**10 Actionable Items for Daily Clarity:**

1. Morning Mindfulness: Start each day with 5-10 minutes of mindful breathing or meditation.

2. Mindful Transitions: Take three deep breaths between tasks to reset your mind.

3. Nature Breaks: Spend at least 15 minutes daily in nature, even if it's just sitting by a window.

4. Tech-Free Time: Designate 1-2 hours daily as device-free to reduce mental clutter.

5. Emotion Labeling: When strong emotions arise, name them silently to yourself.

6. Gratitude Journal: Each night, write down three things you're grateful for.

7. Single-Tasking: Focus on one task at a time, giving it your full attention.

8. Mindful Listening: In conversations, listen without planning your response.

9. Body Scan: Before bed, do a quick mental scan of your body to release tension.

10. Reflection Time: Weekly, reflect on what clouded your mind and what brought clarity.

**20 Self-Reflection Questions to assess your level of inner serenity and clarity:**

1. How often do I feel truly present in the moment?

2. When was the last time I felt a sense of mental clarity?

3. What thoughts or worries most frequently cloud my mind?

4. How do I typically respond to emotional turmoil?

5. Can I recall a time when a clear mind helped me make a wise decision?

6. How often do I practice mindfulness or meditation?

7. What is my relationship with technology? Does it enhance or hinder my mental clarity?

8. How do I feel after spending time in nature?

9. Can I listen to others without internally formulating my response?

10. How often do I take breaks during the day to reset my mind?

11. Do I have a regular practice for processing emotions?

12. How do I nurture my relationships when my mind is clear?

13. What activities make me lose track of time (in a good way)?

14. How do I react when faced with unexpected challenges?

15. Can I observe my thoughts without getting entangled in them?

16. How often do I express gratitude?

17. Do I multitask frequently? How does it affect my peace of mind?

18. What is one small step I can take today towards mental clarity?

19. How might my life change if I consistently cultivated a clear mind?

20. What wisdom or insight has my clear mind revealed to me recently?

Reflecting on these questions can deepen your understanding and commitment to maintaining a clear mind. Remember, this journey is not about perfection but about continuous, compassionate awareness. Each step you take towards clarity ripples out, touching not just your life but the lives of all you encounter. In a world that often feels chaotic, your clear mind is a beacon of peace, a gift to yourself and to all.

# References to Neuroscience Topics and Concepts in Chapter 18: Reflections of a Clear Mind: A Journey to Inner Serenity

1. Prefrontal cortex activity in long-term meditators: Research shows increased activity in the brain's prefrontal region among individuals who practice meditation regularly over extended periods.

2. Brain regions associated with attention, emotional regulation, and self-awareness: The prefrontal cortex is involved in higher-order cognitive functions including focusing attention, managing emotions, and maintaining self-awareness.

3. Amygdala activation during negative emotions: The amygdala, a key component of the brain's emotional processing system, becomes more active when a person experiences negative emotions.

4. Shift in brain activity when labeling emotions: When people consciously identify and name their emotions, brain activity tends to shift from emotional centers to areas associated with rational thinking.

5. Concept of "mindsight" in modern psychology: "Mindsight" refers to the ability to observe and understand one's own mental processes with clarity and compassion.

6. Effects of mindfulness training on working memory and reading comprehension: Studies indicate that practicing mindfulness can improve cognitive functions such as working memory and reading comprehension.

7. Reduced activity in the subgenual prefrontal cortex after nature walks: Spending time in nature, even brief walks, has been shown to decrease activity in brain areas associated with negative rumination.

8. Brain's "fight or flight" center (amygdala): The amygdala plays a crucial role in processing fear and initiating the body's stress response.

9. Neuroscience of mind-wandering: Researchers study the brain processes involved when attention drifts from the present moment to unrelated thoughts or memories.

10. Brain activity during rumination and negative moods: Certain areas of the brain, particularly in the prefrontal cortex, show increased activity during persistent negative thinking or rumination.

# Chapter 19
# Energy, passion, resilience

As I sit here, pondering the beautiful tapestry of life that you and I are weaving, I am struck by the profound interplay of energy, passion, and resilience. These three elements are not just abstract concepts but the very essence of our existence, intricately woven into the fabric of our daily lives. Let's embark on a journey together to explore how these forces can transform your life, drawing insights from the fascinating field of neuroscience and real-life stories that will resonate with your unique experiences.

**Energy: The Spark of Life**

Imagine a morning when you wake up feeling refreshed, your mind clear and your body vibrant. This is the magic of positive energy at work. Neuroscientists have discovered that our brains are wired to seek out and amplify positive experiences. This phenomenon, known as "experience-dependent neuroplasticity," means that the more we focus on positive energy, the more our brains become attuned to it (Hanson, 2013).

Take Meena, a freelance graphic designer. She used to start her days sluggishly, dragging herself to her desk.

Then, she learned about the power of morning rituals. She began each day with a 10-minute meditation, followed by a brisk walk in the park. Neuroscience tells us that meditation increases activity in the left prefrontal cortex, associated with positive emotions and resilience (Davidson et al., 2003). And that walk? It floods her brain with endorphins and BDNF (brain-derived neurotrophic factor), a protein that helps grow new neurons (Cotman & Berchtold, 2002).

The result? Meena now greets her work with curiosity and enthusiasm. She finds herself taking on challenging projects that once seemed daunting. Her energy has become a magnet, attracting clients who value her innovative spirit. This is the power of positive energy – it doesn't just make you feel good; it transforms the quality of your work and relationships.

But what about those days when energy feels low? Remember, it's natural. Our brains have a negativity bias, an evolutionary trait that once kept us alert to dangers (Baumeister et al., 2001). The key is not to fight this bias but to gently redirect it. Try the "Three Good Things" exercise: each night, write down three positive things that happened. This simple act shifts your brain's focus, reinforcing neural pathways associated with optimism (Seligman et al., 2005).

## Passion: The Heart's Compass

Now, let's talk about passion. It's more than just a fleeting interest; it's what gives your life depth and meaning. Neuroscience reveals that when we engage in activities we're passionate about, our brains release a cocktail of feel-good neurotransmitters: dopamine (motivation), serotonin (well-being), and oxytocin (connection) (Achor, 2010).

Consider the story of Sanjoy, a corporate lawyer who secretly loved photography. For years, he suppressed this passion, believing it was impractical. But the long hours and unfulfilling work took their toll. His wife noticed his dimming spark and encouraged him to take a weekend photography course. The effect was immediate. In that class, surrounded by like-minded people, Sanjoy's brain lit up. fMRI studies show that when we engage in activities we love, multiple brain regions activate in a harmonious dance (Gollub et al., 2013).

Inspired, Sanjoy started waking up an hour earlier to photograph the sunrise. He joined a local photography club. His passion didn't just make his weekends richer; it spilled over into his work. He began seeing his legal cases through a new lens, finding creative angles he'd never noticed before. His clients and colleagues remarked on his renewed energy.

Your passion might be gardening, writing poetry, or solving puzzles. Whatever it is, make time for it. It's not a luxury; it's a necessity for a rich, meaningful life. And here's a beautiful secret: passion is contagious. When you share your enthusiasm, you activate mirror neurons in others, allowing them to experience a shadow of your joy (Rizzolatti & Craighero, 2004). By honoring your passions, you create a ripple effect of positivity.

Resilience: The Soul's Bounty

Life, with all its beauty, also brings challenges. This is where resilience shines. It's not about avoiding hardship but about bouncing back, sometimes even growing stronger. Neuroscience shows that resilience isn't a fixed trait; it's a skill we can cultivate (Southwick & Charney, 2012).

Meet Aisha, a small business owner. When the pandemic hit, her café, her labor of love, had to close. She was devastated. But Aisha didn't crumble. She remembered an article about post-traumatic growth - the idea that trauma can lead to positive change (Tedeschi & Calhoun, 2004). She started calling her regular customers, not to sell, but to connect. She learned their stories, their struggles. This act of reaching out activated her ventral striatum, a brain area linked to altruism and resilience (Telzer et al., 2011).

Inspired by these conversations, Aisha pivoted. She started a meal delivery service, focusing on comfort foods that nourished both body and soul. Her customers, touched by her resilience, spread the word. Within months, her business was thriving in a new form. Aisha's story teaches us that resilience isn't about going it alone. Social connection, gratitude, and finding meaning in adversity are key (Masten, 2001).

We all have this strength within us. When faced with a setback, try the "ABCDE" method: Adversity (what happened), Beliefs (your thoughts about it), Consequences (how you feel/act), Disputation (challenging negative thoughts), and Energization (the positive outcome) (Seligman, 2011). This cognitive reframing strengthens neural pathways associated with optimism and problem-solving.

Bringing It All Together

Energy, passion, and resilience are not isolated traits but a symbiotic trinity. Your energy fuels your passions, your passions give you the resilience to overcome obstacles, and your resilience replenishes your energy. This cycle, grounded in neuroscience, is the key to a life of vibrancy and fulfillment.

Remember, you are on a unique journey. These words are not just ink on paper but a heartfelt message from one soul to another. Embrace your energy, cherish your passions, and cultivate your resilience. In doing so, you aren't just improving your life; you're contributing to a more energized, passionate, and resilient world.

**Here are 10 actionable ideas to practice and increase energy, passion and resilience:**

1. Start your day with a mindfulness practice (meditation, yoga, or deep breathing) to boost positive energy.

2. Take a daily nature walk to increase BDNF and endorphins.

3. Practice the "Three Good Things" exercise every night to rewire your brain for optimism.

4. Schedule weekly time for your passion, treating it as non-negotiable self-care.

5. Share your passion with others to spread joy and strengthen social bonds.

6. When faced with a challenge, use the ABCDE method to build resilience.

7. Engage in random acts of kindness to boost your ventral striatum activity.

8. Join a community related to your interests for support and inspiration.

9. Keep a "resilience journal" to track your growth through adversities.

10. End each day with a gratitude meditation to strengthen neural pathways of well-being.

**20 questions for self-assessment and reflection to see where you stand on energy, passion and resilience:**

1. How do I currently start my day, and how can I infuse more positive energy into my mornings?

2. When was the last time I felt truly energized? What was I doing, and how can I incorporate more of that into my life?

3. What activities make me lose track of time? How can I prioritize these passions?

4. How do I respond to setbacks? Do I see them as failures or opportunities for growth?

5. Who are the people that uplift my energy? How can I spend more quality time with them?

6. What negative self-talk patterns do I notice? How can I challenge and reframe these thoughts?

7. How has a past adversity made me stronger? What did I learn from it?

8. When I imagine my most fulfilling life, what passions are at the center of it?

9. How do I recharge when my energy is low? Are these methods truly restorative?

10. In what ways do I share my passions with others? How does this affect my relationships?

11. What daily habits might be draining my energy? How can I reduce or eliminate them?

12. How has focusing on gratitude changed my perspective on challenges?

13. When I feel resilient, what physical sensations do I notice in my body?

14. How can I make my physical environment more conducive to positive energy?

15. What would I do differently if I knew I couldn't fail? How can I bring that boldness into my life now?

16. How do I celebrate small wins? Am I acknowledging my progress enough?

17. What new skill or knowledge would energize me to learn?

18. How can I use my passions to contribute positively to my community?

19. When I'm in a resilient mindset, how does it affect my decision-making?

20. If energy, passion, and resilience were people, what would they say to me right now?

Reflecting on these questions will deepen your understanding of how energy, passion, and resilience interplay in your unique life. Remember, every small step you take nurtures the vibrant, passionate, and resilient soul that you are. Your journey is a beautiful unfolding, guided by the wisdom of your mind, the fervor of your heart, and the strength of your spirit.

# Neuroscience Concepts in Chapter 19: Energy, Passion, and Resilience

1. Experience-dependent neuroplasticity:

The brain's ability to strengthen positive experiences through focus. This concept suggests that the more we concentrate on positive energy, the more our brains become attuned to it (Hanson, 2013).

2. Meditation's effect on the left prefrontal cortex:

Research indicates that meditation increases activity in the left prefrontal cortex, which is associated with positive emotions and resilience (Davidson et al., 2003).

3. Exercise and its effects on the brain:

Physical activities like walking flood the brain with endorphins and BDNF (brain-derived neurotrophic factor), a protein that helps grow new neurons (Cotman & Berchtold, 2002).

4. Negativity bias:

An evolutionary trait of the brain that keeps us alert to dangers. This bias is a remnant of our evolutionary past that once served a crucial survival function (Baumeister et al., 2001).

5. Neurotransmitters released during passionate activities:

When we engage in activities we're passionate about, our brains release a cocktail of feel-good neurotransmitters: dopamine (motivation), serotonin (well-being), and oxytocin (connection) (Achor, 2010).

6. Brain activation during loved activities:

fMRI studies show that when we engage in activities we love, multiple brain regions activate in a harmonious dance (Gollub et al., 2013).

7. Mirror neurons:

These neurons are activated when sharing enthusiasm, allowing others to experience a shadow of your joy. This phenomenon contributes to the contagious nature of passion (Rizzolatti & Craighero, 2004).

8. Ventral striatum activation:

This brain area is linked to altruism and resilience. It's activated by acts of reaching out to others, suggesting a neurological basis for the resilience-building effects of social connection (Telzer et al., 2011).

9. Cognitive reframing:

Techniques like the "ABCDE" method (Adversity, Beliefs, Consequences, Disputation, Energization) can strengthen neural pathways associated with optimism and problem-solving (Seligman, 2011).

10. Post-traumatic growth:

This concept suggests that trauma can lead to positive change in the brain, highlighting the brain's capacity for resilience and adaptation in the face of adversity (Tedeschi & Calhoun, 2004).

11. Resilience as a skill:

Neuroscience shows that resilience isn't a fixed trait but a skill we can cultivate (Southwick & Charney, 2012).

12. Social connection and resilience:

Research indicates that social connection, gratitude, and finding meaning in adversity are key components of resilience (Masten, 2001).

13. Positive psychology exercises:

Practices like the "Three Good Things" exercise can shift the brain's focus, reinforcing neural pathways associated with optimism (Seligman et al., 2005).

This compilation of neuroscience concepts illustrates the intricate relationship between our brain's functioning and the experiences of energy, passion, and resilience. It underscores how our daily practices and mental attitudes can shape our neural pathways, influencing our overall well-being and capacity to thrive in the face of challenges.

# Chapter 20
# Experiencing deepest form of love: A Journey to the Heart's Deepest Chamber

In the tapestry of human emotions, love stands out as the most vibrant and cherished thread. Yet, as you've so eloquently observed, what often passes for love is but a pale imitation—a tangled web of attachment, desire, and conditional affection that can unravel at the slightest tug. Today, I invite you on a journey to explore a rarer, more profound form of love that transcends these superficial bonds. This is the love that sustains us, heals us, and ultimately, defines our humanity.

Imagine a love so pure that it seeks nothing in return, a love that persists. This is the deepest form of love, a selfless devotion aimed solely at the well-being of the beloved. It's a love that sees beyond the surface, beyond the changeable moods and circumstances, to the eternal essence of a person—their soul. This love is not a fleeting emotion but a steady, nurturing presence that permeates every action and intention.

Let's consider the story of Maria and her mother, Genevieve. Genevieve had struggled with addiction for years, her behavior often hurtful and unpredictable.

Many would have given up on her, but not Maria. Even when Genevieve's actions pushed everyone away, Maria's love remained steadfast. She didn't condone her mother's behavior but saw it as a symptom of deep pain. Maria's love manifested in tireless efforts to help her mother heal—arranging therapy, being a shoulder to cry on, and always reminding Genevieve of her inherent worth. After years of struggle, Genevieve finally found sobriety. She credits Maria's unwavering love as the light that guided her out of darkness. This is the transformative power of unconditional love.

Neuroscience offers fascinating insights into this profound love. Studies show that when we love deeply and unconditionally, our brains release a cocktail of chemicals—oxytocin, dopamine, and serotonin—that not only make us feel good but also reduce stress and promote healing. Dr. Barbara Fredrickson, a leading positive psychology researcher, calls this "positivity resonance." It's a synchronous exchange of biochemical and behavioral cues between people that fosters mutual care, concern, and affection.

But here's the truly remarkable part: the benefits of giving such love are as profound as receiving it. A study published in the journal "Psychoneuroendocrinology" found that participants who practiced compassionate meditation (focusing on warmth and care for others) had lower levels of the stress hormone cortisol and a stronger immune response compared to those who didn't. In other words, loving others unconditionally is good for our own health!

This aligns with the wisdom of great spiritual traditions. The Dalai Lama often speaks of compassion as the source of both individual and societal well-being. Similarly, in the Christian tradition, agape love—selfless, unconditional love—is considered the highest form of love, exemplified by Christ's sacrifice.

But unconditional love isn't limited to grand gestures or spiritual figures. It's in the everyday actions of people like Venkat, a teacher in a challenging small-town school. Many of his students come from troubled homes and act out in class. Yet, Venkat greets each child with warmth and patience. He believes in their potential even when they don't believe in themselves. Over time, his unwavering positive regard transforms his classroom. His students begin to trust, to engage, to believe in their own worth. Venkat's love doesn't depend on his students' behavior or achievements; it's a constant that allows them to grow.

This kind of love also manifests in friendships. Consider Lila and Sami, friends since childhood. When Sami confided in Lila that he was gay, he feared rejection. But Lila's love didn't falter. She stood by him through the challenges of coming out, offering support when he faced discrimination. Her love wasn't contingent on Sami fitting societal norms; it celebrated his authentic self. Years later, when Lila's business failed and she fell into depression, Sami was her rock. Their bond, forged in unconditional acceptance, proved unbreakable.

Now, you might wonder, "Can I cultivate this kind of love? Is it a rare gift, or can it be nurtured?" The beautiful truth is that the capacity for unconditional love resides in all of us. It's not about being a saint or never feeling hurt or anger. It's about a commitment to seeing the inherent dignity in every person, to acting from a place of compassion even when it's hard.

Neuroscientist Richard Davidson's research on long-term meditators shows that practices like loving-kindness meditation can actually rewire our brains, strengthening circuits associated with empathy and compassion. This suggests that unconditional love is a skill we can develop, much like learning a language or a musical instrument.

But it doesn't require hours of meditation. Small, daily acts can cultivate this love. It's about pausing before reacting in anger, trying to understand the pain behind someone's hurtful behavior. It's about offering a kind word to a stranger, or really listening when a friend speaks, without judgment or the need to fix. It's about forgiving, not because the other person deserves it, but because holding onto resentment only hardens our own hearts.

Remember, this love starts with self. Many of us are our own harshest critics, withholding from ourselves the compassion we freely give others. But as the saying goes, you can't pour from an empty cup. Loving yourself unconditionally—acknowledging your flaws with gentleness, celebrating your strengths without arrogance—creates a wellspring from which you can nourish others.

This journey to unconditional love isn't always easy. There will be times when you feel drained, when your love seems unappreciated or taken for granted. But here's the miracle: true unconditional love is never depleted. As you give it, you find more within yourself. It's like the story of the widow in ancient scriptures who, despite having almost nothing, shared her last bit of oil and flour. Miraculously, her jars remained full. So it is with love given freely—it multiplies, it sustains, it comes back to you in ways you might never expect.

In our fast-paced, often divisive world, cultivating this love is more than personal growth—it's a radical act of healing. Imagine if we approached conflicts, whether personal or global, from this place of unconditional regard for each other's humanity. The ripple effects would be profound.

I invite you to embark on this journey. Start small, be patient with yourself, and watch as your capacity to love deeply transforms not just your relationships, but your very experience of life. In the quieter moments, you'll find a joy that doesn't depend on external circumstances, a peace that comes from knowing you're contributing to the world's healing, one act of love at a time.

Remember, in a universe vast and often mysterious, our ability to love unconditionally might just be our greatest gift. It's the light we're called to shine, no matter how dark the night. And as you shine it, trust that somewhere, someone is being warmed by your glow.

**10 Actionable Items for Daily Practice on Cultivating Unconditional Love:**

1. Start each day with a self-compassion mantra, like "I am worthy of love and kindness."

2. Practice active listening in one conversation daily, focusing solely on understanding, not responding.

3. Perform one random act of kindness for a stranger each day.

4. When faced with someone's hurtful behavior, pause and silently wish them well before reacting.

5. Keep a "Gratitude and Beauty" journal, daily noting one thing you're grateful for and one beautiful quality you observed in someone.

6. Spend 5 minutes daily in loving-kindness meditation, directing good wishes to yourself, a loved one, a neutral person, and someone who has hurt you.

7. Before bed, forgive yourself for one "mistake" or perceived shortcoming from the day.

8. Choose one relationship to focus on each week, making a conscious effort to express unconditional positive regard.

9. When giving compliments, focus on the person's inherent qualities rather than achievements.

10. At the end of each day, reflect on one way you extended or received unconditional love.

**20 self-reflection questions to assess your progress on unconditional love:**

1. Can I recall a time when someone loved me unconditionally? How did it feel?

2. Do I find it easier to love others unconditionally or to love myself this way?

3. What fears or beliefs might be holding me back from loving more deeply?

4. How do I typically react when someone I love disappoints me? Is this reaction aligned with unconditional love?

5. Can I think of a time my love was conditional? What can I learn from that experience?

6. How often do I judge others? Can I transform that judgment into understanding?

7. Do I ever use my love as a bargaining tool or withdraw it as punishment?

8. How do I treat myself when I make mistakes? Would I treat a dear friend the same way?

9. Have I ever experienced the "healing power" of unconditional love, either giving or receiving it?

10. How might my relationships change if I committed to seeing the "beauty of the soul" in everyone?

11. Do I believe that unconditional love can coexist with healthy boundaries? How?

12. When was the last time I forgave someone who hadn't apologized? How did it affect me?

13. How often do I take time to really celebrate the unique essence of my loved ones?

14. Can I love someone deeply while disagreeing with their actions or beliefs?

15. How has my understanding of love evolved over my lifetime?

16. Do I ever withhold love from myself or others as a form of self-protection? Is it truly protecting me?

17. How might practicing unconditional love change my experience of loneliness or rejection?

18. What role models of unconditional love do I have in my life or in history? What can I learn from them?

19. How could embracing unconditional love make me a force for healing in my community?

20. If I knew I could never be depleted by giving love, how would I love differently today?

Reflecting on these questions can deepen your understanding and practice of unconditional love. Remember, this isn't about achieving perfection but about setting your heart's compass towards this profound love. Each step, each kindness, each moment of understanding brings you closer to experiencing the richest, most resilient joy humans can know—the joy of loving without condition. Your journey to this love is perhaps the most important voyage you'll ever undertake.

**Neuroscience Topics and Research in Chapter 20: Experiencing deepest form of love: A Journey to the Heart's Deepest Chamber**

1. Brain Chemistry of Love

- The brain releases a combination of chemicals during deep, unconditional love:

- Oxytocin

- Dopamine

- Serotonin

- These chemicals are associated with positive feelings and stress reduction.

2. Positivity Resonance

- Concept introduced by Dr. Barbara Fredrickson, a leading positive psychology researcher

- Described as a synchronous exchange of biochemical and behavioral cues between people

- Fosters mutual care, concern, and affection

3. Compassionate Meditation and Stress Reduction

- Study published in the journal "Psychoneuroendocrinology"

- Findings:

- Participants practicing compassionate meditation had lower levels of cortisol (stress hormone)

- These participants also showed a stronger immune response compared to non-meditators

4. Brain Plasticity and Compassion

- Research by Neuroscientist Richard Davidson

- Focus: Long-term meditators

- Findings: Practices like loving-kindness meditation can rewire the brain

- Specifically strengthens circuits associated with empathy and compassion

5. Neuroplasticity in Love and Compassion

- The ability to develop unconditional love is likened to learning a skill

- Suggests that the brain can be trained to enhance capacity for empathy and compassion

6. Neuroscience of Self-Compassion

- Self-love is important for brain health and overall well-being

## Chapter 21
## A transformative journey of the soul

As I sit here, writing this chapter, I am filled with a profound sense of warmth and connection. This message comes from a place of deep care and understanding. The journey of personal transformation is not just a path you walk alone, but one that resonates with the very essence of our shared human experience.

We often find ourselves caught up in the whirlwind of daily life - the deadlines, the responsibilities, the constant stream of information. In this rush, it's easy to forget that beneath all these layers lies a profound truth: the core purpose of our life is personal transformation and evolution into a better being. This isn't just a lofty philosophical idea, but a tangible reality backed by scientific research and countless personal stories.

Let's start by understanding what we mean by transformation. It's not about changing who you fundamentally are, but rather about uncovering and nurturing the beautiful, resilient soul that resides within you. Your soul has an incredible capacity for unconditional love. It's like a wellspring of compassion that, when tapped into, can transform not just your life but also uplift those around you.

Consider the story of Anna, a nurse in a busy city hospital. Every day, she faced challenging situations - patients in pain, overworked colleagues, and the constant pressure of life-and-death decisions. Initially, she found herself becoming cynical and detached, a common response to such stress. But then, she discovered mindfulness meditation. Through this practice, Anna began to reconnect with her innate capacity for compassion. She realized that her job wasn't just about administering medications or changing bandages; it was about being a source of comfort and strength for her patients.

Neuroscience supports Anna's experience. Studies using functional MRI scans have shown that practices like meditation activate regions in the brain associated with empathy and compassion, such as the anterior cingulate cortex and the insula. One study by researchers at the University of Wisconsin-Madison found that even short-term compassion training increased altruistic behavior and neural responses to suffering. In essence, by nurturing her soul's capacity for love, Anna transformed her work from a job into a calling.

But transformation isn't just about our souls; it's also about our emotions. We all experience a spectrum of feelings, from the shadow of anger and resentment to the light of joy and gratitude. The key is not to eliminate negative emotions - they are part of being human - but to transform how we respond to them.

Take the case of Sundar, a young entrepreneur. His startup failed after years of hard work, leaving him with debts and a sense of failure. Anger, jealousy towards successful peers, and resentment towards investors who pulled out consumed him. His negative emotions were understandable, but they were also holding him back.

Sundar's turning point came when he started practicing gratitude journaling, a technique studied extensively in positive psychology. Each night, he wrote down three things he was grateful for. At first, it felt forced. But gradually, he began to appreciate the lessons from his failure, the skills he had gained, and the resilience he had developed.

A study published in the Journal of Personality and Social Psychology found that people who regularly practiced gratitude experienced more joy, optimism, and satisfaction with their lives. They also had fewer physical complaints and exercised more. For Sundar, this practice didn't erase his past, but it transformed his emotional landscape. His anger softened into determination, his jealousy into inspiration to learn from others' successes.

Now, let's talk about the body. We often view the body merely as a machine that needs maintenance. But the body is so much more - it's a vehicle for enriching life, a vessel for transformative journey.

Consider Sumati, a corporate lawyer with a sedentary lifestyle. Long hours at her desk led to chronic back pain, poor sleep, and constant fatigue. She saw her body as a hindrance, something that was failing her. Then, she discovered yoga. At first, she approached it as just another exercise routine. But as she delved deeper, she realized yoga was transforming her relationship with her body.

Through yoga, Sumati learned to listen to her body's needs, to respect its limits, and to marvel at its capabilities. She found that certain poses eased her back pain better than any medication. More profoundly, the mindful breathing in yoga started to calm her racing mind. A study in the International Journal of Yoga found that regular yoga practice leads to significant improvements in cognitive function, including attention, processing speed, and executive function.

For Sumati, her body transformed from a source of frustration to a partner in her wellbeing. She started taking walking meetings, energizing both her body and her work interactions. She introduced short meditation breaks in her team, boosting collective focus and creativity. Her physical transformation rippled out, enhancing not just her life but her entire workplace.

These stories – Anna's, Sundar's, and Sumati's - underline a beautiful truth: realizing the full potential of a human life and its ability to transform is its true purpose. This isn't about achieving some external measure of success. It's about the inner journey of uncovering your soul's capacity for love, transforming your emotional responses, and partnering with your body in this grand adventure.

Now, I want to outline something tangible, a roadmap for our own transformative journey.

**Here are 10 actionable items, each backed by science and real-life examples, that you can easily incorporate into your daily routine:**

1. Mindful Morning Minutes: Start your day with 5-10 minutes of mindfulness meditation. Like Anna, you'll activate your brain's compassion centers. Divya, a schoolteacher, found that these morning minutes made her more patient with her students, transforming her classroom into a more nurturing environment.

2. Gratitude Journaling: Each night, write down three things you're grateful for. Sundar's story shows how this can shift your emotional baseline. Richa, a single mom, found that focusing on gratitude helped her appreciate her children's small victories, making parenting more joyful.

3. Body Check-Ins: Set reminders to check in with your body every 2 hours. Notice any tension, hunger, or need for movement. Tushar, a programmer, used this to prevent eye strain and wrist pain, making his work more sustainable and enjoyable.

4. Compassion Practice: Each day, consciously send good wishes to someone, even someone who annoys you. A study in the Journal of Happiness Studies found this reduces stress and increases feelings of connection. Mala, a customer service rep, used this to stay calm with difficult clients, improving her job satisfaction.

5. Nature Connection: Spend at least 15 minutes in nature daily. Research shows this reduces stress hormones and boosts mood. Ajay, an accountant, started having lunch in a nearby park. He found that this "green time" refreshed his problem-solving skills.

6. Mindful Eating: For one meal a day, eat without distractions. Savor the flavors and textures. Studies show this improves digestion and satisfaction. Nayan, a busy executive, found that mindful eating helped her make healthier food choices and enjoy meals more.

7. Movement Breaks: Take a 5-minute movement break every hour. This could be stretching, a short walk, or some yoga poses. Rahul, a copywriter, found these breaks

enhanced his creativity, making writer's block a thing of the past.

8. Bedtime Reflection: Before sleep, reflect on one way you showed or received kindness today. This reinforces your soul's capacity for love. Samantha, a nurse like Anna, found this practice helped her find meaning even on tough days.

9. Learning Time: Dedicate 30 minutes a day to learning something new that excites you. Neuroplasticity research shows this builds cognitive resilience. Zubin, a retiree, started learning guitar. This new skill brought joy and connected him with a community of music lovers.

10. Act of Random Kindness: Each week, perform one unexpected kind act. It could be as simple as a genuine compliment. Studies show that kindness is contagious. Indu, a college student, started leaving encouraging notes for classmates. This transformed her dorm's atmosphere to one of mutual support.

These actions aren't just tasks; they're invitations to transform. Each one is a step towards realizing your soul's capacity for love, transforming your emotions, and partnering with your body. They're backed by science, but more importantly, they're validated by real people's lives.

**Now, to help you reflect on your own transformative journey, here are 20 questions. Take time with each one. They're not just questions, but portals to deeper self-understanding:**

1. When was the last time you felt truly at peace? What contributed to that feeling?

This question helps you identify sources of peace in your life, guiding you to cultivate more of these moments.

2. Can you recall an instance when you responded to anger with compassion? How did it change the situation?

Reflecting on this builds your capacity to transform anger into understanding, a key aspect of emotional growth.

3. What daily habit makes you feel most connected to your body?

This question encourages mindfulness of physical practices that enrich your life.

4. Who in your life has shown you unconditional love? How has it impacted you?

Recognizing received love helps you understand and extend this soul-nurturing gift to others.

5. When you feel jealous, what story are you telling yourself? Is it true?

This question challenges negative self-narratives, a first step in transforming jealousy into self-acceptance.

6. How often do you consciously express gratitude? How does it affect your mood?

Regular reflection on gratitude reinforces its power to shift your emotional landscape.

7. Can you think of a recent challenge that, in hindsight, helped you grow?

This reframes difficulties as opportunities for transformation, building resilience and optimism.

8. When was the last time you did something kind for your body?

This promotes viewing your body as a partner in wellbeing, not just a machine to be maintained.

9. How has helping others changed your perspective on your own problems?

Acts of kindness often provide perspective, transforming personal worries into broader compassion.

10. What negative emotion do you struggle with most? Have you tried to understand its root?

Understanding emotions' origins is key to transforming them, as seen in research on emotional intelligence.

11. Can you recall a time nature soothed your stress? How can you incorporate more "green time"?

This reinforces the transformative power of nature connection, backed by studies on eco-therapy.

12. How often do you pause to celebrate small victories? Does it boost your motivation?

Acknowledging progress, no matter how small, can transform your journey from a chore to a joyful process.

13. When you're kind to strangers, how does it make you feel? Why do you think that is?

This question taps into the reciprocal nature of kindness, shown in studies on altruism and wellbeing.

14. How has learning something new changed your self-perception?

Learning boosts confidence and cognitive health, transforming your sense of potential at any age.

15. Can you think of a repeated negative thought? How might you rephrase it compassionately?

This practice, core to cognitive-behavioral therapy, transforms harsh self-talk into self-compassion.

16. When did you last feel deeply understood? How can you offer that understanding to others?

This promotes empathetic listening, a transformative act that strengthens all relationships.

17. How does your energy change after mindful breathing? Why do you think that happens?

This raises awareness of meditation's physiological benefits, encouraging regular practice.

18. Can you recall a moment of pure joy? What senses were engaged?

Sensory mindfulness enhances joy, transforming ordinary moments into sources of delight.

19. How has showing vulnerability transformed a relationship in your life?

Vulnerability, though scary, often deepens connections, transforming superficial ties into genuine bonds.

20. When you picture your most transformed self, what are you doing? How can you start today?

This vision aligns your daily actions with your deepest aspirations, making transformation tangible.

Each of these questions is a mirror, reflecting aspects of your transformative potential. They touch on the interplay of soul, emotions, and body. They remind you that transformation isn't a distant goal, but a journey you're already on, with each mindful breath, each act of kindness, each moment of self-compassion.

You are not alone on this journey. Every person you meet is on their own path of transformation. By realizing your potential - your soul's capacity for love, your ability to transform emotions, your body's role in enriching life - you don't just elevate yourself. Like ripples in a pond, your transformation touches everyone around you.

In the hustle of daily life, it's easy to forget this grand purpose. But I hope this book serves as a gentle reminder. May it be a lantern on your path, illuminating the transformative potential in each moment, each interaction, each breath.

You are on a magnificent journey. A journey of uncovering the love within your soul, of alchemizing emotions into wisdom, of partnering with your body in this dance of life. It's a journey worthy of your full engagement, your deepest care.

So, take a deep breath. Feel the air transforming within you, nourishing every cell. And know that with each such breath, each act of kindness, each moment of self-reflection, you're not just living. You're transforming. You're realizing the true, beautiful purpose of your human life.

**Neuroscience Research References in Chapter 21: "A transformative journey of the soul"**

1. Functional MRI scans show that meditation activates brain regions associated with empathy and compassion, such as:
 - Anterior cingulate cortex
 - Insula

2. Study by researchers at the University of Wisconsin-Madison:
 - Finding: Short-term compassion training increased altruistic behavior and neural responses to suffering

3. Research on gratitude:
 - Published in: Journal of Personality and Social Psychology
 - Finding: Regular gratitude practice correlates with increased joy, optimism, and life satisfaction

4. Yoga and cognitive function:
 - Published in: International Journal of Yoga
 - Finding: Regular yoga practice leads to significant improvements in cognitive function, including attention, processing speed, and executive function

5. Nature and stress reduction:
 - Finding: Spending time in nature reduces stress hormones and boosts mood

6. Mindful eating:
- Eating without distractions improves digestion and satisfaction

7. Neuroplasticity:
- Learning new skills builds cognitive resilience

8. Kindness and social contagion:
- Acts of kindness have a contagious effect in social settings

9. Emotional intelligence:
- Concept: Understanding the origins of emotions is key to transforming them

10. Eco-therapy:
- Concept: Nature connection has therapeutic effects

11. Altruism and well-being:
- Concept: Acts of kindness benefit both the giver and receiver

12. Cognitive-behavioral therapy:

- Technique: Rephrasing negative thoughts compassionately

13. Mindful breathing and physiological effects:
- Concept: Meditation has observable effects on the body

14. Sensory mindfulness and joy:
- Concept: Engaging multiple senses can enhance experiences of joy

www.ingramcontent.com/pod-product-compliance
Lightning Source LLC
LaVergne TN
LVHW061606070526
838199LV00078B/7197